No Babies!

No Marriage!

Until we are Free!

The Movement to take back our rights

by Maraina Marrion Vegadose

Title: No Babies! No Marriage! Until we are Free! : The Movement to take back our rights
Author: Maraina Marrion Vegadose
Publisher: Northwest Evergreen Holdings

ISBN: 9798345850381

First Edition: October 2024

This is dedicated to all the women who have been lost.

Index

Foreword

As you open this book, you are joining a movement—one that is not only for women but for every person who believes in the sanctity of human dignity, autonomy, and freedom. At the heart of this work lies a simple yet powerful truth: the right to control one's own body is the most fundamental of all rights. Without it, any promise of liberty or equality is incomplete, an aspiration never fully realized.

For over two centuries, the ideals of freedom and personal sovereignty have been woven into the fabric of America's identity. We celebrate the principles of life, liberty, and the pursuit of happiness, but these principles have been unevenly applied. Women, in particular, have long been denied full ownership of their bodies—subjected to laws, customs, and ideologies that prioritize control over their autonomy.

This book is a call to action, a demand that we recognize bodily autonomy as the bedrock of true freedom. It explores not only the struggles faced by women but the broader human rights implications that arise when anyone's body becomes subject to external control. The concepts ahead are a deep dive into the philosophical, historical, medical, and societal issues that have led us to this point, examining why reproductive rights and personal sovereignty are not just "women's issues" but matters that affect the core of our shared humanity.

It is also a reflection on the many voices—religious, political, and cultural—that have perpetuated these struggles.

1

Yet, it also points toward hope and change, showing us how other societies, traditions, and movements have embraced equality and autonomy, leading to greater freedom, healthier families, and more just communities.

Whether you are a woman fighting for the right to control your body, a man standing with those whose freedoms are restricted, or simply a citizen who believes in justice and equality, this book is for you. It is a roadmap to understanding how deeply intertwined personal autonomy is with the promises of liberty and human dignity. And, most importantly, it is a guide to reclaiming the rights that have always belonged to us.

As you turn these pages, I invite you to reflect on the stakes, the history, and the future we can build together. This movement is not only about individual freedom but about creating a society where everyone—regardless of gender—can live fully, freely, and with the dignity that every human deserves.

The future of freedom is in our hands. Let us claim it, together.

Introduction: The Call for a Revolution of Bodily Autonomy

In a nation built on the ideals of freedom and self-determination, American women find themselves facing a grave injustice: the continued denial of full bodily autonomy. Despite the progress made over centuries, the government and political institutions still hold undue power over our most fundamental possession—our bodies. Today, we are proposing a radical but necessary action: a marriage and birth strike, a movement of collective refusal until we secure a constitutional amendment that guarantees every woman complete control over her body.

This proposal is not without precedent. In South Korea, women are currently on a marriage and birth strike in response to the extreme misogyny they face in their society. Tired of systemic oppression, they have refused to participate in a system that devalues them, withholding their reproductive labor as a form of protest. The results have been striking—South Korea's birth rate has plummeted to the lowest in the world, forcing the government to reckon with the cost of ignoring women's rights. The South Korean women's strike has demonstrated the power of collective action in challenging patriarchal systems. And here in the United States, we can do the same.

The need for this strike becomes clearer when we examine the current political climate. Across the country, restrictive abortion laws have been passed in rapid succession, severely limiting women's access to reproductive healthcare. The 2022 overturning of *Roe v. Wade* opened the floodgates for states to enact harsh abortion bans, with little regard for the physical and emotional toll it places on women. In states like Texas, where abortion is now illegal after six weeks—often before many women even know they are pregnant—women are being forced to carry pregnancies to term against their will, even in cases of rape, incest, or severe fetal abnormalities.

These government restrictions are not only wrong; they are causing real, measurable harm. Women are already responding to this assault on their rights by making drastic decisions—choosing sterilization over the risk of pregnancy in a country where they cannot safely access abortion. In fact, demand for sterilization procedures, such as tubal ligations, has surged in states with restrictive abortion laws, as women feel they have no other option to protect their autonomy. Faced with the possibility of forced childbirth, many women are opting to never have families at all, making the painful but necessary choice to prioritize their bodily safety over the potential joys of motherhood.

This trend is having a profound impact on America's birth rate, which was already in decline. In 2020, the U.S. birth rate reached its lowest point in decades, with 56 births per 1,000 women of childbearing age. The recent wave of anti-abortion laws has only accelerated this decline. Experts predict that these policies will decimate the birth rate further, exacerbating an already shrinking population. This will have long-lasting economic and social consequences, from a reduced labor force to strained support systems for the elderly.

At the same time, the cost of living continues to soar, and the traditional two-parent income household is no longer sufficient to meet basic needs. In 2022, inflation in the United States reached its highest level in 40 years, driving up the cost of everything from housing to healthcare. The median price for a home in the U.S. is now over $400,000, and rent prices have skyrocketed nationwide. Many families, even with two working adults, are finding it nearly impossible to make ends meet. As a result, more and more households are relying on the incomes of four or more adults to survive. Experts forecast that by the end of this decade, it may become common for households to require five incomes just to cover the basics—food, shelter, and healthcare.

These economic realities paint a grim picture of what it means to bring a child into the world today. Raising a family in an environment of financial precarity, political instability, and shrinking reproductive rights is not only difficult—it is a recipe for generational harm. Yet, the government and religious institutions insist on framing forced birth as a moral necessity, ignoring the suffering it inflicts on both women and the children born into these dire conditions.

This brings us to the heart of the matter: the fundamental right of bodily autonomy. The human body must be recognized as the sole property of the person inhabiting it. The government, the church, and any other institution have no right to make decisions about an individual's body. This is not merely a question of reproductive rights; it is a question of ownership and self-governance. Our bodies are not vessels to be commandeered by politicians or religious leaders; they are ours, and we alone must have the right to decide what happens to them.

For centuries, women have fought for the right to control their own bodies, and for centuries, they have been denied full autonomy. Even Christianity, which is often cited in defense of forced birth, has a complex history when it comes to reproductive rights. Early Christian sects, such as the Cathars, believed that bringing children into a world full of suffering was itself an act of cruelty. They discouraged marriage and childbearing, recognizing the immense moral weight of procreation in a harsh, unkind world.

Furthermore, the Bible itself contains texts that show the early Hebrew approach to suspected pregnancies resulting from infidelity. In Numbers 5:11-31, there is a ritual that ends suspected illegitimate pregnancies—evidence that even in religious contexts, terminating a pregnancy was considered justifiable under certain conditions. This casts doubt on the modern church's claim that it has always been pro-life. In fact, the church has historically been more concerned with growing its membership than with preserving life. For 2,000 years, the Catholic Church has taken lives over heresy, witchcraft, and disobedience, yet it now claims moral authority over the most intimate aspects of women's lives.

The hypocrisy of the church is clear: its position is not truly pro-life, but pro-birth. It is a position driven by the need for more parishioners, more power, and more control. And in this pursuit, the church has ignored the real suffering caused by forced birth, overpopulation, and the deprivation of women's rights.

This is why we call for a revolution of bodily autonomy. The American woman must take control of her future, just as the women in South Korea are doing. We must refuse to participate in a system that denies us the most basic of human rights—the right to our own bodies. This movement is not just about abortion or contraception; it is about demanding that the government and religious institutions step back and recognize that our bodies are ours alone. Only then can we achieve true equality and freedom.

We will explore the philosophical, legal, historical, and medical evidence for why bodily autonomy must be enshrined in the Constitution. We will draw on the works of Enlightenment thinkers, indigenous legal traditions, and religious movements that support the claim that the human body is inviolable. We will also offer an action plan for collective resistance, showing how women can use their power to force the necessary constitutional change.

This is not just a call to action—it is a call for liberation. The time has come for American women to rise up and demand the freedom that has been denied to us for far too long.

Chapter 1: The Body as Sacred Property – Reclaiming Our Inviolable Rights

In the heart of the American experiment, there exists a singular promise that has echoed through the centuries: the right to freedom. From the days of the Founding Fathers, the pursuit of life, liberty, and happiness has been the core of the nation's identity. The Constitution, that living document crafted by visionaries, enshrines these ideals and offers protection to all American citizens. But while our papers, our homes, and our effects are secured by the Fourth Amendment, there remains an overlooked truth—that the most personal and sacred property we possess, our bodies, has never been fully shielded by the law.

The Founders believed in the sanctity of personal property, and in this belief, they crafted the Fourth Amendment to protect citizens from unwarranted searches and seizures, ensuring the security of one's home and possessions. Yet, the human body, the very vessel through which we experience life and exercise freedom, remains unprotected to the fullest extent. If our homes are sanctuaries that the government cannot invade without due cause, how much more sacred should the body be—the vessel that houses our very being?

The time has come to recognize that the human body must be regarded as an individual's property in the most fundamental sense. It is not merely a vessel but the very foundation of personal liberty. To make decisions about one's body, free from government intrusion or coercion, is to fulfill the deepest promise of American freedom. This right cannot be left to the ambiguity of interpretation; it must be etched into the highest law of the land. A constitutional amendment guaranteeing full bodily autonomy is the only way to ensure that the most personal of all possessions—the body—belongs solely to its inhabitant.

Philosophical Foundations of Bodily Autonomy

The idea that the body is the ultimate form of property is not new. It is rooted in the Enlightenment ideals that helped shape the very foundation of the American republic. John Locke, one of the most influential thinkers of the time, declared that every person has a "property" in their own body. In his *Second Treatise of Government*, Locke argued that the natural rights of man included the right to life, liberty, and property. He believed that our bodies, like our labor and possessions, are extensions of our personal sovereignty. If we cannot claim ownership over our own bodies, what other freedom can we truly possess?

Mary Wollstonecraft, a contemporary of Locke and a champion of women's rights, took this idea even further. In her revolutionary work, *A Vindication of the Rights of Woman*, she argued that the same rights and freedoms extended to men should apply to women, particularly the right to self-governance. To her, autonomy over one's own body was a critical part of human dignity. She called upon society to recognize that denying women control over their own bodies was a profound violation of their natural rights.

Classical Greek philosophers, such as Socrates and Aristotle, laid the groundwork for the concept of individual choice and governance. Aristotle's *Politics* and *Nicomachean Ethics* explored the idea that self-determination was essential to human flourishing. He argued that a life worth living was one where the individual was free to make choices regarding their own body and mind, without interference from external authorities.

These Enlightenment and classical ideals shaped the very spirit of America. The Founders themselves, in their letters and personal writings, often referenced these thinkers. Thomas Jefferson, in his correspondence, frequently invoked Locke's concept of natural rights. In a letter to James Madison, Jefferson reflected on the importance of securing these fundamental rights, including the "pursuit of happiness"—a phrase that implicitly called for bodily autonomy as the cornerstone of human freedom.

Yet, despite their lofty ideals, the Founders did not fully account for the autonomy of women's bodies in their vision of freedom. The Constitution they drafted laid the groundwork for a nation, but it left critical gaps that would take centuries to address. The abolition of slavery, the granting of voting rights to women, and civil rights legislation all represented steps toward a fuller realization of freedom. Now, we must take the next step: enshrining the right to one's own body as a constitutional guarantee.

The American Tradition of Expansion

The United States has always been a work in progress, constantly evolving to more fully realize its promise of liberty. The expansion of rights over time is a testament to the strength of the American spirit. Just as previous generations fought to include marginalized voices in the definition of "We the People," we must now demand that the body—the most sacred property we possess—be granted its rightful protections under the law.

Without an amendment that guarantees full bodily autonomy, we risk betraying the very principles upon which this nation was founded. The government must not have the power to dictate what a person can or cannot do with their own body. It is a violation of the core American belief in individual liberty, and it is a breach of the social contract that exists between the government and its citizens.

In the words of Percy Shelley, "Man must be free, or he is not man." This sentiment, though written over two centuries ago, rings truer today than ever before. Freedom, in its truest form, includes the right to make decisions about one's own body, free from coercion or interference. Shelley believed in radical individualism—the idea that each person must have the ability to govern their own life, unencumbered by the will of others.

Now is the time for us to stand on the shoulders of these great thinkers and demand what is rightfully ours. The body must be recognized as the ultimate form of property, and the freedom to govern it must be enshrined in the Constitution. Only then can we fulfill the promise of American liberty and live in a society that respects the most fundamental human right—the right to our own bodies.

The Limitations of the Fourth Amendment

While the Fourth Amendment of the U.S. Constitution promises protection against unreasonable searches and seizures, it has proven insufficient in shielding the autonomy of our bodies. It protects our homes, papers, and effects from government intrusion—but not our bodies in the most crucial aspects. This fundamental omission has led to centuries of legal and social battles in which women, in particular, have struggled to maintain control over their own reproductive rights and bodily autonomy.

Court cases over the years, including *Roe v. Wade* and *Planned Parenthood v. Casey*, have highlighted the tension between bodily autonomy and government authority. These cases, though crucial to advancing reproductive freedom, were only temporary victories. With the overturning of *Roe v. Wade* in 2022, it became painfully clear that the protection of bodily autonomy could be eroded as easily as it was established through legal precedent. The erosion of these rights underscores the need for a definitive constitutional amendment that protects all bodies from undue governance.

The body is not merely an extension of property rights; it *is* property in its most personal form. To treat it as anything less is to deny the individual the most basic and profound of freedoms: the right to self-determination. Without the explicit protection of an amendment that guarantees the inviolability of one's body, any other liberties guaranteed by the Constitution can be hollow.

Why an Amendment Is Necessary

A constitutional amendment is more than a legal change; it is a cultural and moral declaration that we, as a society, believe in the absolute sovereignty of the individual over their own body. This amendment must be unequivocal in its language and comprehensive in its scope, recognizing the right of every person to make decisions about their own body without interference from the state, corporations, or any other entity.

Historically, amendments to the Constitution have been used to correct societal wrongs and expand rights that should have been enshrined from the beginning. The Thirteenth Amendment abolished slavery, the Nineteenth granted women the right to vote, and the Civil Rights Act of 1964 addressed racial inequalities. Just as those amendments addressed grave injustices, so too must we now amend the Constitution to protect the bodily autonomy of every person. Anything less is a failure to honor the full meaning of freedom.

An amendment would provide an unassailable foundation for personal autonomy. It would create legal safeguards that no future court could easily dismantle, offering lasting protection for generations to come. This amendment must be grounded not only in the principles of liberty but also in the philosophical and ethical arguments that have long championed individual sovereignty.

The Philosophical Case for Bodily Autonomy

In calling for this amendment, we stand on the shoulders of giants—philosophers and thinkers who, for centuries, have argued that the individual's body is the most sacred and inviolable form of property. John Locke, perhaps the most influential philosopher of the Enlightenment, stated that "every man has a property in his own person. This nobody has a right to but himself." Locke's assertion that personal liberty and bodily autonomy are inextricably linked forms the very foundation of the natural rights doctrine upon which the United States was built.

But Locke was not alone. Mary Wollstonecraft, writing in the 18th century, recognized that women, in particular, were denied autonomy over their own bodies and lives. Her call for equality, for the recognition that women are rational beings with the right to self-governance, laid the intellectual groundwork for future movements advocating for women's rights. Her vision of an enlightened society included the idea that without control over one's body, all other freedoms are meaningless.

Even further back, the Greek philosopher Epicurus argued that the pursuit of happiness—one of the ideals upon which the American Constitution was founded—was inherently linked to the freedom of the individual to make choices about their own body. In his view, bodily autonomy was not merely a legal issue but a moral one. To deny someone the right to their own body was to deny them the pursuit of a fulfilled life.

In more recent times, Simone de Beauvoir, a key figure in existentialist philosophy and feminist thought, contended that a woman's body has been historically seen as property—something to be controlled by others. De Beauvoir argued for women's liberation from this ownership, recognizing that autonomy over one's body is the first step toward true freedom.

From these philosophical foundations, we draw the strength and clarity to demand the ultimate legal recognition of bodily autonomy. The framers of the Constitution were heavily influenced by the works of Locke, Montesquieu, and Rousseau, all of whom championed individual freedom. We, too, must follow in that tradition by extending the promise of liberty to the most fundamental realm of existence—the human body.

The American Spirit of Progress

The very essence of America is its ability to evolve and expand its notion of freedom. Our nation's history is one of expanding the circle of rights, of breaking down barriers, and of advancing the cause of liberty. In that spirit, we call upon Americans to recognize that the battle for bodily autonomy is the next frontier of freedom. Just as we abolished slavery and granted women the right to vote, we must now enshrine in the Constitution the right of every individual to have sovereignty over their own body.

The Founders did not have all the answers; they left the Constitution open to amendment for a reason. They understood that their document was a framework, a starting point from which future generations could build a more just and equitable society. Now it is our turn to build upon that foundation. It is our turn to expand the promise of freedom to include the most personal and sacred possession we have—our own bodies.

A New Declaration of Independence

We, as American citizens, must declare that our bodies are our own. This is not a radical demand, but a fulfillment of the very principles upon which our country was founded. To deny anyone the right to their own body is to deny them the most basic of freedoms. It is time for us to recognize that freedom does not truly exist without bodily autonomy, and it is time for the Constitution to reflect that truth.

This new declaration of independence, this call for an amendment guaranteeing full bodily autonomy, is not only a moral imperative but a patriotic one. For in securing the right to our own bodies, we are securing the future of liberty in America. We are ensuring that the promise of freedom, so eloquently penned in 1776, is fully realized for all people. The body is not just property—it is the foundation of freedom itself. And it must be protected.

Chapter 2: Reclaiming the Sacred Role – The Fight for Equality in the Church

From the earliest days of human civilization, religion has played a central role in shaping societies, guiding moral compasses, and defining gender roles. In the Christian tradition, however, there exists a buried truth—a truth of equality that was once central to the faith but was systematically erased over the centuries. Contrary to the patriarchal structures we often see in modern religious institutions, women once stood side by side with men in the ministry of Jesus and the early church. They were leaders, teachers, ministers, and disciples, entrusted with the same spiritual responsibilities as their male counterparts. The suppression of women's voices within the church is a betrayal of the very message of inclusivity and equality that Jesus himself preached.

Early Christian teachings embraced the equality of women, how religious sects such as the Gnostics and the Cathars continued this tradition, and how the church's later leaders stripped women of the power and authority they were meant to share. It is a call to remember that, in the eyes of Jesus, women were not only equals but essential leaders in the faith—a truth that modern women must reclaim.

Jesus and the Women of His Ministry

The story of Jesus Christ is one of radical inclusion and compassion, transcending the rigid boundaries of gender, class, and status that defined his time. Jesus not only welcomed women into his circle of disciples, but he also granted them roles that were revolutionary for a patriarchal society.

One of the most compelling examples of Jesus' commitment to gender equality can be found in the figure of Mary Magdalene. Often misrepresented by later church leaders as merely a repentant sinner, Mary was, in fact, one of Jesus' most devoted and trusted disciples. In the *Gospel of John*, she is the first to witness the resurrection of Christ, a moment of profound theological significance. This was no accident—Jesus chose to reveal his resurrected self to a woman, entrusting her with the critical task of delivering the good news to the other disciples. In doing so, he shattered the traditional gender roles of his time, elevating Mary Magdalene to a position of spiritual leadership.

Mary's role as a disciple and leader is further evidenced by the discovery of the *Gospel of Mary*, an ancient text that was excluded from the canon by the early church. In this gospel, Mary Magdalene plays a prominent role in teaching the other disciples, a clear indication that she was viewed as more than just a follower. She was a minister in her own right, offering spiritual guidance and interpreting Jesus' teachings. That her gospel was later suppressed by the institutional church speaks to a deliberate erasure of women's leadership roles within early Christianity.

Jesus' inclusivity did not stop with Mary Magdalene. Throughout the New Testament, we see him engaging with women in ways that were unheard of for a Jewish man in first-century Palestine. He spoke to the Samaritan woman at the well, breaking both gender and ethnic taboos. He healed women, defended them from unjust punishment, and praised their faith, often elevating them above his male disciples in their understanding of his message. In these actions, Jesus laid the groundwork for a church that was meant to include women as equals, not subordinates.

The Early Church and Female Leadership

After Jesus' ascension, the early Christian community continued this radical inclusivity. Women played a significant role in the spread of Christianity, serving as deacons, apostles, and leaders of house churches. In the writings of the apostle Paul, we find references to several prominent women in the early church, including Phoebe, who was a deacon in the church at Cenchreae, and Junia, who is described as "outstanding among the apostles" in Romans 16:7. These titles were not merely honorary; they denoted real positions of authority within the Christian community.

The early church was, by necessity, a decentralized and often underground movement, and women were crucial in its expansion. They hosted gatherings in their homes, taught new converts, and administered the sacraments. The equality of women in the early church was not only a spiritual ideal but also a practical reality. However, as Christianity became institutionalized and aligned with political power, this equality began to erode.

The Suppression of Women's Roles in the Church

The fourth century marked a turning point in the history of the church, as Christianity became the official religion of the Roman Empire. With this newfound status came the formalization of church structures and the consolidation of male authority. The Council of Nicaea in 325 AD, and subsequent councils, began the process of defining orthodoxy and church hierarchy, systematically excluding women from positions of leadership.

This was not simply a shift in policy but a theological redefinition of gender roles. Church fathers such as Augustine and Tertullian argued that women were inherently inferior to men, both physically and spiritually, using scripture to justify their claims. These teachings reinforced the patriarchal structures of the time and led to the gradual erasure of women's contributions to the early church. By the Middle Ages, the idea of women serving as ministers, deacons, or apostles had been all but obliterated from mainstream Christian practice.

However, not all Christians accepted this new hierarchy. The Gnostics, a sect that emerged in the early centuries of Christianity, continued to ordain women as ministers and recognized their spiritual authority. In Gnostic texts, such as the *Gospel of Thomas*, women are depicted as equal to men in their pursuit of spiritual enlightenment. One famous Gnostic saying from this gospel states that Jesus told his disciples, "Every woman who makes herself male will enter the kingdom of heaven," a metaphorical way of suggesting that gender distinctions have no place in spiritual matters.

The Gnostics were not alone. The Cathars, a Christian sect that flourished in the 12th and 13th centuries, also embraced the equality of women within their religious community. In Catharism, women could be "perfects," a term used for those who had achieved spiritual enlightenment and were qualified to lead their congregations. This stood in stark contrast to the Catholic Church of the same period, which had fully embraced a male-only priesthood and relegated women to the status of passive followers.

The Struggle for Equality in Modern Christianity

The suppression of women's roles in the church has persisted for centuries, but the struggle for equality has never truly ended. In the modern era, women have continued to fight for their rightful place in Christian leadership. The ordination of women in many Protestant denominations, as well as the rise of female ministers in non-denominational churches, represents a partial restoration of the equality that existed in the early church.

Yet, the battle is far from over. The Catholic Church, with its vast global influence, continues to deny women the right to ordination. This denial is rooted in centuries of patriarchal tradition, not in the teachings of Jesus. It is a reflection of the institutional church's fear of losing power, rather than a reflection of the true message of the Gospel.

Reclaiming the Church Jesus Gave to Women

To truly reclaim the equality Jesus offered women, we must look back to the roots of Christianity, to the time when women were leaders, apostles, and teachers. The early church was not a place of exclusion; it was a place of radical inclusion, where women and men worked side by side to spread the message of Christ. This is the church we must strive to rebuild—a church where women are recognized not as mere followers but as equals in the ministry of Jesus.

We must remember that it was not Jesus who took power from women; it was the later church leaders who did so in an attempt to consolidate their own authority. Jesus' message was one of equality, compassion, and love—values that cannot coexist with the subjugation of half the human race. By recognizing this truth, we can begin to restore the balance that was lost and work toward a church that truly reflects the inclusivity Jesus envisioned.

In this effort, we find allies in history. The Gnostics, the Cathars, and countless other marginalized Christian groups have kept alive the tradition of female equality, even in the face of persecution. Their example, along with the teachings of Jesus himself, provides the foundation for a new movement toward equality within the church—a movement that must also extend beyond the walls of the church into the broader struggle for women's rights and autonomy.

A Call to Reclaim the Church for All

As we move forward, it is crucial to remember that the fight for women's equality within the church is not a new one. It is a fight that began with Jesus himself, who saw no difference between the worth of men and women. It is a fight that has continued through the centuries, carried on by groups like the Gnostics and the Cathars, who refused to bow to the patriarchal forces that sought to silence them.

Now, in the 21st century, it is time for us to reclaim the church that Jesus envisioned—a church where women are not only welcomed but empowered to lead. The message of the Gospel is one of liberation, and that liberation must include the right of every woman to share fully in the ministry and leadership of the church.

By reasserting the role of women in the church, we not only honor the true teachings of Jesus, but we also strike a blow against the forces of oppression that have long sought to keep women in subjugation. The time has come for the church to return to its roots and embrace the equality that was always meant to be at its core. In doing so, we take one more step toward the larger goal of full autonomy and equality for women everywhere.

From the earliest days of Christianity, women have played critical roles in shaping the faith, standing side by side with men in the ministry of Jesus. However, over time, women were stripped of the positions of authority and leadership that were meant for them. We will examine the historical and theological foundations of female equality in the Christian tradition, how the institutional church stripped away that equality, and how key religious leaders—many of them men—have long argued for the restoration of women's rightful place in the church.

These voices, many of them prominent priests, theologians, and preachers, remind us that the suppression of women in the church was not part of Jesus' plan but rather a distortion introduced by later church authorities. These men saw the vision of Jesus clearly—one where women were central to the ministry, spiritual leaders, and equals. Their voices give us the authority to reclaim what was lost and challenge the current structures of religious oppression.

Jesus and the Early Church's Radical Inclusion

As we have established, the early ministry of Jesus was one of radical inclusion. Jesus entrusted women with leadership roles, most notably Mary Magdalene, whom he chose to witness and proclaim his resurrection. The writings that later became excluded from the canon, such as the *Gospel of Mary*, underscore the prominent role women were meant to play in the early church. Jesus' decision to elevate women to such key roles broke with the patriarchal customs of the time, signaling that his message was not confined by the social norms of gender.

The Church's Shift and the Suppression of Women's Roles

Despite this, the church, as it institutionalized in the centuries following Christ's death, systematically dismantled the equality that women held in the early Christian community. By the time of the Roman Empire's adoption of Christianity, patriarchal structures had begun to replace the inclusive and equal teachings of Jesus. In particular, women were increasingly barred from roles of religious leadership, their voices silenced in public worship and their rights restricted.

The suppression of women's roles in the church came to a head in the writings of influential early theologians like Tertullian and Augustine, who upheld patriarchal interpretations of scripture. However, not all church fathers were proponents of this exclusion. There were key voices throughout history that consistently called for the restoration of women's leadership roles in the church, asserting that equality was not only scriptural but also a reflection of God's will.

Prominent Christian Leaders Advocating for Equality

1 **Gregory of Nazianzus (4th Century AD)**
Gregory of Nazianzus, one of the great Cappadocian Fathers of the early church, was a defender of women's intellectual and spiritual capacity. In his writings, he expressed admiration for his sister Macrina, who was a theologian and teacher in her own right. Gregory's view on women was radical for his time, as he believed in their equal ability to teach and lead:

"Women, in the true sense, can be men in spirit.
Those who show greater understanding are seen
to lead."

Gregory's belief in the intellectual and spiritual equality of women made him a rare voice in the early church and laid a foundation for later Christian leaders who would advocate for women's roles in the church.

2 **John Wesley (1703-1791)**
John Wesley, the founder of Methodism, was a strong advocate for the role of women in the ministry. In a time when many Protestant denominations still limited women's involvement, Wesley allowed women to preach and lead within the Methodist movement.

Wesley recognized that women, just like men, could be called by God to share the Gospel. In a letter to the Countess of Huntingdon, he wrote:

"What reason can there be why a woman should not be a witness for Christ just as a man is? When women are filled with faith and the Holy Spirit, ought not they to preach as well as men?"

Wesley's advocacy for women's spiritual equality marked a turning point in Protestantism and opened the door for women to take leadership roles within many branches of the Christian faith.

3 **Charles Haddon Spurgeon (1834-1892)**
Known as the "Prince of Preachers," Charles Spurgeon, a renowned Baptist preacher, was ahead of his time in supporting women's contributions to ministry. Though Spurgeon operated within a largely conservative tradition, he believed in the capacity and calling of women to serve in leadership roles within the church:

"We must acknowledge that many women possess abilities which would well qualify them for the ministry… Why should it be deemed unlawful for a woman to preach or to speak when she speaks with wisdom, zeal, and grace?"

Spurgeon, though revered for his deep theological insight, was also willing to break with the more rigid traditions of his time to defend women's ability to preach and lead within the church.

26

4 **William Booth (1829-1912)**

William Booth, the founder of the Salvation Army, was an outspoken advocate for women's rights within both society and the church. Booth saw no distinction between men and women when it came to spreading the gospel, and he actively promoted women into leadership roles within his organization. Booth's wife, Catherine Booth, was a co-leader of the movement, and Booth himself believed strongly in the equality of women:

"Some of my best men are women!"

Booth's leadership in the Salvation Army was revolutionary in its approach to gender equality, allowing women to serve as ministers and commanders in equal standing with men. His example has continued to influence denominations that recognize women's leadership today.

5 **Karl Barth (1886-1968)**

Karl Barth, one of the most influential theologians of the 20th century, also spoke on the equality of women, particularly in their role as teachers and leaders in the Christian community. Barth's theological work on the doctrine of creation emphasized the equal dignity and worth of men and women in the eyes of God. He asserted that both genders were created in the image of God, and thus both were called to participate fully in the life of the church.

"Man and woman are equally made in the image of God… The Church cannot deny women their place at the heart of Christian ministry without denying the very teachings of Christ."

Barth's deep theological influence spread across Protestantism, challenging traditional views of gender and encouraging a more inclusive understanding of leadership within the Christian faith.

Other Voices of Equality

Beyond these prominent figures, there are countless other male Christian leaders who have called for equality within the church. Dietrich Bonhoeffer, a German theologian and anti-Nazi dissident, believed in the importance of women's roles in Christian ministry. He wrote that the suppression of women's voices in the church was a tragedy and a loss to the faith. More recently, Pope Francis has spoken about the importance of women's contributions to the church, stating that "a church without women is like the apostolic college without Mary."

These leaders, spanning different denominations and centuries, consistently point to a deeper truth: that gender equality in the church is not only compatible with Christian teachings but is a necessary part of living out the message of Christ. Their voices stand as a reminder that the struggle for equality is not a new one—it is deeply rooted in Christian history.

The Cathars and Gnostics: A Tradition of Equality

Beyond mainstream Christian voices, groups such as the Gnostics and Cathars embraced gender equality as a central tenet of their faith. The Cathars, in particular, who flourished in the 12th and 13th centuries, practiced a form of Christianity where women and men shared equal roles in leadership and spiritual authority. Women served as "perfects" in the Cathar tradition, leading communities and administering sacraments.

The Gnostics also elevated women to positions of spiritual leadership. Their texts, such as the *Gospel of Mary* and the *Gospel of Thomas*, reveal a worldview where the distinctions between male and female were irrelevant in the pursuit of spiritual truth. In Gnosticism, spiritual enlightenment was accessible to all, regardless of gender.

These alternative Christian sects, though often persecuted and marginalized by the institutional church, remind us that there has always been a tradition of equality within Christianity—one that we must now reclaim.

Reclaiming the True Church of Equality

The teachings of Jesus were always meant to empower women and bring them into full participation in the Christian ministry. As history shows, it was not Christ, but later church authorities who suppressed the voices of women and denied them their rightful place in the church. From Gregory of Nazianzus to John Wesley, Charles Spurgeon, William Booth, and Karl Barth, male leaders have long recognized that women have an equal role to play in spreading the Gospel and leading Christian communities.

Now, in the 21st century, it is time to fully embrace this truth and restore the equality that was once central to the Christian faith. Women were always meant to lead in the church, just as they did in the days of Jesus. To deny them that role is to deny the very teachings of Christ himself.

By drawing upon the wisdom and authority of Christian leaders throughout history, we can make the case that women are not only deserving of equality in the church—they are essential to its future. The struggle for gender equality in the church is not new, but it is a struggle we must continue with the authority of those who have come before us and with the knowledge that we are carrying forward the true spirit of the Gospel.

Christianity's Inherent Call for Women's Equality

Christianity, at its core, is a faith built upon the principles of love, compassion, and justice. Jesus' teachings repeatedly emphasized the inherent dignity and worth of every individual, transcending the boundaries of class, race, and, most importantly, gender. In his ministry, Jesus not only included women but elevated them to positions of spiritual leadership, challenging the societal norms of his time. The early church followed his example, with women serving as apostles, deacons, and teachers, contributing equally to the spread of the Gospel.

To deny women equal rights and choices, including control over their own bodies and governance over their own lives, is to deny the very teachings of Jesus Christ. Christianity has never been about the domination of one group over another but about the liberation and empowerment of all. Throughout history, Christian leaders—Gregory of Nazianzus, John Wesley, Charles Spurgeon, William Booth, and Karl Barth—have upheld the biblical truth that women and men are equals in the eyes of God, deserving of equal authority within the church and society.

The exclusion of women from leadership and decision-making, especially regarding their own bodies, is a distortion introduced by later church authorities who sought to consolidate their power rather than live out the radical inclusivity of Jesus' message. It is an injustice rooted not in scripture but in human failing, and it must be corrected.

As Christians, we are called to follow the example of Christ, who granted women an equal voice and welcomed them as indispensable contributors to his mission. This equality extends not only to their roles in the church but also to their fundamental rights over their bodies and their lives. To ignore this truth is to turn away from the message of the Gospel.

Just as Jesus stood for the oppressed and the marginalized, we too must stand for the equality of women in every aspect of life—spiritually, socially, and legally. Christianity, when properly understood, demands nothing less. Women are deserving of the same rights, the same choices, and the same governance over their bodies and lives as men. This is not only a moral imperative but a reflection of the justice, love, and equality that lie at the very heart of the Christian faith.

To argue against the equality of women within Christianity, in their rights over their own bodies and their governance over their lives, is to argue against the teachings of Jesus himself. And that, for any Christian, should be an impossible position to hold.

Chapter 3: The Hypocrisy of Pro-Birth – Catharism, the Early Church, and the Cruelty of Forced Birth

Throughout its history, the Christian church has proclaimed itself as a defender of life, but closer examination reveals a complex and often hypocritical relationship with the sanctity of life. While modern Christian institutions, particularly those within the Catholic tradition, have positioned themselves as "pro-life," opposing birth control and abortion, their historical actions and doctrinal inconsistencies paint a different picture—one that often places institutional growth over true compassion for human suffering.

The early Christian sect of the Cathars provides a compelling counter-narrative to this stance. The Cathars, who flourished in southern France during the 12th and 13th centuries, believed that the material world was inherently corrupt and cruel. For them, bringing children into a world marked by suffering and hardship was an act of injustice. We will explore how the Cathar view on marriage, childbirth, and suffering directly challenges the modern church's rigid pro-birth stance, exposing its deeper motivations of control and institutional expansion. By drawing on the historical actions of the church, from executions for heresy to the horrors of forced birth under famine and overpopulation, we will reveal the hypocrisy of the so-called "pro-life" position.

The Cathars and the Cruelty of Childbearing

The Cathars, a Gnostic Christian sect, held beliefs that were deeply at odds with the mainstream Catholic Church. They viewed the physical world as a place of suffering, corruption, and decay, created by an evil force. For the Cathars, salvation was found in rejecting the material world and seeking spiritual purity, which included abstaining from marriage and procreation. They believed that bringing new life into a world filled with suffering and moral corruption was an act of cruelty.

According to surviving accounts of Cathar practices, many adherents chose celibacy and discouraged childbearing. In their view, procreation merely perpetuated the cycle of suffering. The Cathar clergy, known as "perfects," were often celibate and promoted a life free from the material burdens of this world. They argued that, given the inevitability of suffering, it was morally wrong to bring new lives into such a brutal existence.

This belief system may seem extreme to modern ears, but it holds a kernel of truth that resonates with current concerns about overpopulation, poverty, and suffering. The Cathars understood that bringing children into a world where they would face hardship, pain, and cruelty was not an act of love or life, but one of perpetuating misery. For them, avoiding procreation was a form of compassion and spiritual wisdom, a stance that stands in stark contrast to the modern church's blanket opposition to birth control and abortion.

The Quaker's views on the creation of family

Quakers, known formally as the Religious Society of Friends, have a deep-rooted tradition of simplicity, nonviolence, and care for the community, which extends to their views on family life and reproduction. Historically, Quakers have emphasized the moral responsibility that comes with bringing children into the world, believing that children should only be born into joyous, loving homes where their physical, emotional, and spiritual needs can be fully met. This reflects the broader Quaker commitment to stewardship and moderation in all aspects of life, including family planning.

One aspect of Quaker tradition involves the practice of celibacy, particularly among early Quaker communities, where some members chose not to marry or have children as an expression of their spiritual discipline and dedication to living simply. This wasn't a rejection of family life but rather an extension of their belief that all actions, including reproduction, should be undertaken with deep thought and responsibility. Early Quakers believed in the importance of bringing children into a world where they could be nurtured properly and into homes that were ready to provide love, care, and spiritual guidance.

Moreover, adoption has also played a significant role in Quaker history. Quakers have long believed in the importance of providing for orphaned or abandoned children, viewing the act of raising and caring for these children as equally—if not more—important than biological parenthood. This practice aligns with their broader principles of equality and compassion, ensuring that children in need are raised in nurturing environments.

In modern times, Quakers continue to practice moderation when it comes to family planning. They hold the view that creating families should only be done when parents are ready—emotionally, financially, and spiritually—to bring a child into the best possible environment. This cautious approach to reproduction emphasizes that parenthood is a profound responsibility, and it's most godly to wait until the conditions for raising a child are ideal, ensuring the well-being of both the child and the parents.

Quaker teachings on family life remind us that it is not just about bringing children into the world, but about creating homes and environments where those children can thrive. The Quaker belief in inner peace, social justice, and stewardship guides this thoughtful and deliberate approach to family planning, demonstrating that the well-being of the next generation is one of the most sacred duties entrusted to humanity.

The Church's Hypocrisy on Life and Death

The Catholic Church, along with other Christian institutions, has historically been far more concerned with maintaining power and control over its followers than with truly preserving life. Over the centuries, the church has taken countless lives in the name of defending orthodoxy, executing heretics, and waging wars of conquest—all actions that directly contradict its "pro-life" rhetoric.

One need only look at the *Albigensian Crusade* of the 13th century, in which the Catholic Church launched a brutal campaign to eradicate the Cathars. Tens of thousands of men, women, and children were slaughtered for their adherence to a belief system that the church deemed heretical. In a single day during the siege of Béziers, a city that harbored Cathars, the papal legate famously instructed soldiers to "kill them all; God will know his own." This massacre, and countless others like it throughout church history, reveals the church's indifference to life when it conflicts with institutional authority.

Beyond the persecution of heretics, the church has also sanctioned wars, inquisitions, and the systematic oppression of entire populations. The Crusades, the Spanish Inquisition, the Witch Trials—each of these events demonstrates a willingness to take life in the pursuit of religious and political power. The church's history is drenched in blood, undermining its claim to be a protector of life.

The Modern Pro-Birth Agenda: Ignoring Suffering

In its modern "pro-life" stance, the church focuses almost exclusively on preventing abortion and restricting access to contraception, presenting itself as a defender of life from conception to natural death. But this narrative obscures the real consequences of forced birth in a world full of suffering. Just as the Cathars understood centuries ago, bringing children into the world when they are doomed to live in misery—whether due to poverty, war, famine, or abuse—is an act of cruelty, not compassion.

37

Consider the horrific famine in Ethiopia during the latter half of the 20th century, where millions of people faced starvation. Families were forced to watch their children waste away from malnutrition, knowing they could do nothing to save them. In a world where resources are stretched thin, and human suffering is rampant, forcing birth becomes a tool of oppression rather than a celebration of life.

The Catholic Church, along with many other Christian denominations, continues to ignore the reality that overpopulation and extreme poverty exacerbate human suffering on a global scale. In countries already struggling with famine, disease, and violence, the church's opposition to birth control and family planning directly contributes to the misery of millions. By promoting an agenda that opposes contraception and abortion under all circumstances, the church ensures that more children are born into conditions where they are likely to suffer and die prematurely. This is not a defense of life; it is a perpetuation of suffering.

Biblical and Historical Evidence: The Church Was Never "Pro-Life"

To further undermine the modern church's "pro-life" stance, one need only look at its own history and scripture. The Bible contains explicit instructions for dealing with suspected infidelity, including the termination of pregnancies. In the book of *Numbers* (5:11-31), Hebrew law includes a ritual that induces miscarriage if a wife is suspected of being unfaithful. This passage, known as the "ordeal of bitter water," clearly demonstrates that ancient Jewish law allowed for the termination of pregnancy under certain circumstances —far from the absolutist stance taken by the modern church.

Additionally, early Christian sects, including the Cathars and Gnostics, promoted a nuanced view of life and suffering, advocating for the use of spiritual discernment in matters of birth and death. These groups understood that bringing a child into the world without considering the conditions they would face was an act of negligence, not righteousness. In fact, the very survival of the early church was built not on dogma but on adaptability and compassion— values that have been abandoned in favor of rigid pro-birth policies.

The modern church's pro-birth agenda has little to do with the sanctity of life and much to do with maintaining power. By encouraging large families, the church ensures that its congregation continues to grow, filling pews and offering coffers. More parishioners mean more tithes, more influence, and more control. In this sense, the church's stance is not about protecting life but about perpetuating its own power at the expense of human suffering.

The Quakers and Birth Control: A Modern Example of Compassion

In contrast to the Catholic Church's rigid stance, other Christian groups have recognized the moral necessity of birth control and family planning. The Quakers, for example, have long advocated for individual conscience and responsibility in matters of reproduction. As a religious group that values equality, simplicity, and compassion, the Quakers promote family planning as a way to prevent suffering and ensure that children are born into conditions where they can thrive.

The Quakers' approach aligns with the spirit of Jesus' teachings, which emphasize care for the poor, the suffering, and the vulnerable. Rather than forcing women to bear children they cannot care for, the Quakers advocate for responsible parenthood, rooted in compassion and respect for life. Their stance demonstrates that true "pro-life" values include caring for the well-being of both mothers and children, and ensuring that no child is brought into the world only to suffer.

Jesus Would Be for Birth Control

If we take the true spirit of Jesus' teachings to heart—his compassion for the marginalized, his care for the suffering, and his commitment to human dignity—it becomes clear that Jesus would be in favor of birth control. The cruelty of bringing children into a world full of suffering, poverty, and violence is contrary to the values of love and compassion that form the foundation of Christianity.

The modern church's obsession with forced birth ignores the realities of human suffering, perpetuates poverty, and exacerbates overpopulation, all while claiming to defend life. But the historical record shows that the church was never consistently pro-life. Instead, it has often been pro-birth, driven by a desire for control and power, rather than by a true concern for the sanctity of life.

The Cathars, the Quakers, and countless other Christian voices throughout history have recognized the moral complexity of childbirth and the need for compassion in matters of reproduction. These voices remind us that bringing children into a world of suffering is not an act of love but an act of cruelty.

True Christian values demand that we consider the well-being of all people, born and unborn, and that we promote policies—like birth control—that allow for responsible, compassionate, and ethical family planning. This is the message that Jesus himself would support, and it is the message we must embrace if we are to honor the sanctity of life in its truest sense.

Several Christian groups, including the Quakers, Mennonites, Catholics, and Latter-day Saints (Mormons), uphold the principle of moderation in childbearing, emphasizing the importance of ensuring that children are brought into prepared, loving, and capable homes. These religious traditions, while some discourage the use of artificial birth control, share a belief in the responsibility that comes with parenthood and the moral necessity of readiness before bringing new life into the world.

The **Quakers** are particularly known for their emphasis on simplicity, responsibility, and care in family life. Historically, some Quaker communities even practiced celibacy, and many have advocated for adopting orphaned children rather than producing their own. This perspective reflects their belief that it is more important to provide a safe, loving environment than to prioritize biological reproduction. Modern Quakers continue this tradition by encouraging family planning that aligns with readiness, emotionally, financially, and spiritually, to provide the best possible upbringing for children.

In **Catholic teachings**, while artificial contraception is discouraged, there is a strong emphasis on "responsible parenthood." According to the doctrine outlined in *Humanae Vitae*, Catholic couples are urged to consider the well-being of the family, the physical and emotional health of the parents, and the conditions into which they are bringing a child. The Catholic Church teaches that it is not only the act of procreation that matters but the readiness and capacity to nurture the child in a way that honors God's commandment to love and protect life.

Mennonite and **Amish** communities, though traditionally large families are common, also emphasize simplicity and the ability to care for and raise children within the context of a stable, self-sufficient home. These groups believe that children should only be brought into the world when parents are prepared to support them fully, spiritually and materially, mirroring their broader values of moderation and stewardship.

Even within the **Latter-day Saints (Mormons)**, the decision to have children is seen as sacred and personal. Though the LDS Church encourages large families, it also teaches that family planning should be guided by personal prayer and reflection, with the readiness of parents being a crucial factor. Couples are encouraged to have children when they feel spiritually and financially prepared to raise them in a stable, loving environment.

In contrast to strict interpretations of reproductive teachings, these religious groups all share an underlying principle: that bringing children into the world is not just a biological act but a deeply moral and spiritual responsibility. The decision to have children should come from a place of readiness and the ability to provide a supportive and nurturing home, not from societal pressure or doctrinal rigidity.

From a broader perspective, scholars across many faiths, including **Jewish** thought, have debated the commandment to "be fruitful and multiply" (Genesis 1:28). Some modern scholars, particularly in light of today's environmental and social crises, argue that this commandment must be understood in a context that values responsible stewardship of the earth and the creation of families only when the conditions for raising them are right. The obligation to populate the earth has, in many ways, been fulfilled, and there is growing recognition that we must balance this commandment with the need to care for God's creation and avoid overpopulation, which could lead to resource depletion and suffering (Jewish Theological Seminary)(Sefaria)(Jewish Theological Seminary).

In conclusion, reproductive rights can coexist with religious beliefs. In many cases, it is understood that the decision of when and how to have children is deeply personal, often left to the discernment of the individual and their relationship with God. This idea extends to the belief that no being, including God, would wish for endless suffering through overpopulation and environmental destruction. Instead, these traditions remind us that thoughtful and responsible parenthood is a reflection of divine love, care, and moderation.

The Peril to the future of the Church

The sharp decline in church membership in the United States is intricately linked to growing dissatisfaction with the institutionalized misogyny and conservative social doctrines espoused by many religious communities. Over the past several decades, church membership has plummeted, with data showing that in 2020, fewer than half of U.S. adults were members of a religious institution, a stark contrast to the 73% reported in 1937. This decline has been particularly pronounced among young people and women.

One of the core reasons for this exodus is the growing disconnect between modern societal values and the gender hierarchy entrenched within many religious institutions. For example, many conservative churches, such as the Southern Baptist Convention, reinforce rigid gender roles, barring women from leadership positions and insisting on their submission to male authority. These teachings starkly contrast with the ambitions and experiences of modern women, particularly those who are highly educated and value equality in their professional and personal lives. Young women, in particular, find it increasingly difficult to reconcile these archaic beliefs with their lived realities, leading many to leave the church altogether. Nearly four in ten Generation Z women now identify as religiously unaffiliated, a significant departure from older generations where women were more likely to participate in religious life than men.

The exodus isn't limited to women. Many men, particularly those who support gender equality, have also found themselves disillusioned by the church's treatment of women. The rise of politicized rhetoric, including staunch anti-abortion stances and opposition to LGBTQ+ rights, has alienated large swathes of the population. A notable number of people cite the church's negative treatment of women and other marginalized groups as a primary reason for leaving their childhood faith.

For many, the church's refusal to adapt to the changing cultural landscape signals its own downfall. By clinging to outdated, patriarchal structures, religious institutions are driving away both women and men who are intolerant of bigotry. This growing disillusionment can be seen not only in membership decline but also in the shift of societal norms, where religion is increasingly seen as irrelevant or even harmful.

If the church wishes to remain relevant in the future, it must confront its misogynistic past and present, and embrace inclusivity. As many ex-church members argue, the church's teachings should align more with the love, acceptance, and equality that Jesus Christ advocated. This would mean welcoming women into leadership roles, supporting reproductive rights, and affirming the dignity of all individuals, regardless of gender or sexuality. Failure to adapt will likely result in the continued decline of religious institutions, as people flee spaces that no longer reflect their values.

In conclusion, the church's failure to treat women equitably is driving its decline, and without a dramatic shift toward inclusivity, its relevance will continue to wane. Churches that embrace equality and inclusiveness will be those that survive in a world that increasingly values human dignity and love over rigid dogma.

Chapter 4: The Philosophical Foundations of Bodily Autonomy

At the heart of the demand for bodily autonomy lies a long tradition of philosophical thought, one that has shaped modern understandings of individual freedom and the right to self-governance. From the Enlightenment thinkers who laid the groundwork for natural rights and liberty to the ancient Greek philosophers who first contemplated the nature of human freedom, this intellectual lineage provides the foundation for the argument that the human body is the ultimate form of property—owned and governed by no one but the individual inhabiting it.

Many historical figures from the Enlightenment period, such as John Locke, Mary Wollstonecraft, and Percy Shelley, alongside ancient Greek philosophers like Socrates, Plato, and Aristotle are considered the very foundational knowledge that created the Constitution of the United States itself. Their collective works offer a compelling case for why bodily autonomy is a fundamental right that must be enshrined in law.

John Locke: Natural Rights and Property Ownership

John Locke, one of the most influential Enlightenment thinkers, is often credited with developing the modern concept of natural rights, which includes the right to life, liberty, and property. Locke's *Two Treatises of Government* (1689) outlines his belief that all individuals possess certain inalienable rights simply by virtue of being human. Central to his argument is the idea that individuals have a natural right to their own bodies, making them the sole proprietors of their physical selves. This notion of self-ownership forms the foundation for Locke's entire philosophy of government and law.

In Locke's words:

> "Every man has a property in his own person.
> This nobody has any right to but himself."
> (*Second Treatise of Government*, Chapter V).

Locke's argument for property rights is not limited to material possessions but extends to the body itself. He asserts that individuals are born with an intrinsic right to control their own bodies, and by extension, their labor, decisions, and actions. Any infringement on this right is, according to Locke, a violation of natural law.

Locke's philosophy underpins much of modern Western thought on individual rights, especially in the context of bodily autonomy. His emphasis on self-ownership provides a powerful argument for why women should have the exclusive right to make decisions about their reproductive health and bodies. If the body is a form of property that belongs solely to the individual, then no government, religious institution, or external force has the moral or legal authority to control it.

Mary Wollstonecraft: Women's Rights and Equality

While Locke's ideas were groundbreaking, they largely applied to men, as the patriarchal society of his time did not consider women as fully autonomous beings. It was Mary Wollstonecraft, the 18th-century feminist philosopher, who expanded on these ideas to argue for the equality of women. In her seminal work *A Vindication of the Rights of Woman* (1792), Wollstonecraft laid the intellectual groundwork for modern feminism, arguing that women possess the same rational capacities as men and should, therefore, be afforded the same rights and freedoms.

Wollstonecraft wrote:

> "It is justice, not charity, that is wanting in the world!" (*A Vindication of the Rights of Woman*, Chapter II).

Wollstonecraft's demand for justice, rather than charity, encapsulates her argument that women are entitled to the same natural rights as men, including control over their own bodies. She believed that the subjugation of women was not only unjust but also a detriment to society as a whole, as it deprived half the population of the opportunity to fully participate in civic life.

Wollstonecraft's work remains a cornerstone of feminist thought, particularly in its insistence on the bodily and intellectual autonomy of women. Her arguments serve as a direct challenge to any institution—whether governmental or religious—that seeks to control women's reproductive choices. Wollstonecraft understood that without control over their own bodies, women could never achieve true equality.

Percy Shelley: Radical Individualism and Liberty

Percy Bysshe Shelley, the Romantic poet and political thinker, took Locke's and Wollstonecraft's ideas further by emphasizing radical individualism and the sanctity of personal liberty. Shelley, a vocal critic of authoritarianism,

49

believed that the ultimate goal of society should be the liberation of the individual from all forms of oppression. In his political treatise *A Philosophical View of Reform* (1820), Shelley argued that the only legitimate form of government is one that guarantees the freedom of each individual to govern their own life and body.

Shelley's view of liberty was deeply personal. He wrote:

> "The most unfailing herald, companion, and follower of liberty is poverty, and its concomitant, degradation." (*A Philosophical View of Reform*, Chapter II).

Shelley's radical belief in the right to self-determination extended to all areas of life, including the body. He saw any attempt to restrict personal liberty as a form of tyranny, particularly when it came to government interference in matters of personal choice. His works advocated for a society in which individuals had absolute control over their own lives and bodies, free from external coercion.

In Shelley's view, bodily autonomy was not just a matter of personal liberty but a prerequisite for a just society. His ideas resonate strongly with contemporary arguments for reproductive rights, as they highlight the inherent injustice of any system that seeks to control individuals' bodies for political or religious ends.

Ancient Greek Philosophers: Human Freedom, Choice, and Governance

The foundations of Western thought on individual autonomy can be traced even further back to the ancient

Greek philosophers, who were among the first to explore the nature of human freedom, governance, and choice. Socrates, Plato, and Aristotle each contributed to the philosophical understanding of self-governance and individual rights, though their views varied.

Socrates, as documented in Plato's *Apology* and *Crito*, famously argued that the most important aspect of life was the pursuit of moral virtue and the right to make one's own choices, even in the face of societal pressure. His commitment to individual conscience, even in opposition to the state, laid the groundwork for later philosophical arguments about personal freedom.

Socrates' refusal to escape his death sentence, despite the opportunity to do so, illustrates his belief in the inviolability of personal choice:

> "The unexamined life is not worth living."
> (*Apology*, 38a).

Plato, in his *Republic*, took a more complex view of governance, advocating for a system in which philosopher-kings would rule in the best interest of the people. However, Plato also acknowledged the importance of individual virtue and the role of personal choice in achieving a just society. His theory of the tripartite soul, which emphasized the balance between reason, spirit, and desire, reflected an early understanding of the need for individuals to have control over their own lives.

Aristotle, in his *Nicomachean Ethics* and *Politics*, developed a more detailed theory of individual rights and governance. He argued that the good life was one in which individuals were free to pursue happiness and virtue through rational choice. Aristotle's concept of *eudaimonia*—human flourishing—depended on individuals having the freedom to make their own choices about their lives, their labor, and their bodies.

Aristotle wrote:

> "Happiness depends upon ourselves."
> (*Nicomachean Ethics*, Book I).

While Aristotle's views were deeply influenced by the hierarchical society in which he lived, his belief in the importance of individual choice and governance has had a lasting impact on Western thought. The Greek philosophical tradition, with its emphasis on reason, autonomy, and moral responsibility, laid the intellectual groundwork for later Enlightenment thinkers like Locke, Wollstonecraft, and Shelley.

The Modern Implications of These Philosophies

The ideas of Locke, Wollstonecraft, Shelley, and the ancient Greek philosophers form the foundation for modern understandings of individual freedom and bodily autonomy. Their collective works argue that personal liberty, including control over one's own body, is a fundamental right that must be protected against all forms of external interference—whether from the government, religious institutions, or societal pressures.

Today, these philosophical principles are more relevant than ever. As women across the world fight for the right to make decisions about their own bodies, the arguments made by these thinkers offer a powerful defense of bodily autonomy. If the human body is the ultimate form of property, as Locke argued, then it is morally and legally indefensible for any institution to claim authority over it. Wollstonecraft's demand for justice, Shelley's plea for individual liberty, and the ancient Greeks' exploration of freedom all point to one undeniable truth: the body belongs to the individual, and no one else.

The struggle for bodily autonomy is not just a political battle—it is a philosophical one, grounded in centuries of thought about human freedom and dignity. To deny women control over their own bodies is to deny them the most basic form of ownership, and it is a violation of the very principles upon which modern democracy is built. By reclaiming these philosophical foundations, we can strengthen the case for constitutional change and ensure that every individual has the right to govern their own body, free from external control.

No one has the right to use another person's body without their explicit consent. This is a principle that underpins modern ethical thought, legal systems, and human rights. Just as no one can be forced to donate a kidney, liver, or any other organ without their voluntary agreement, no one can be forced to use their body to sustain the life of another being without consent. The same must apply to pregnancy and the use of a woman's body by a fetus. At no point should any external force—government, law, or societal pressure—

have the right to compel a woman to use her body in a way that endangers her life, health, or autonomy.

The biological reality is clear: until a fetus reaches viability, it is entirely dependent on the host body for sustenance, protection, and life itself. This biological relationship, while often viewed through the lens of potential life, can be understood as a parasitic relationship—one in which the fetus draws all necessary resources from the mother without her having the option to end the relationship if she chooses. No parasite, no matter how significant, has the right to the life of its host. In the same way, a fetus does not have a right to use a woman's body against her will, as this would violate the most fundamental principle of bodily autonomy.

Once a fetus reaches viability, it moves beyond this parasitic relationship and becomes capable of sustaining life independently, albeit with the help of medical intervention. It is only at this point that the question of the fetus's rights might be considered. Yet even at viability, the paramount concern must still be the health and life of the mother. A society that values life must protect the life of the mother first and foremost, for without her, there is no future for the child. Viability is a threshold for considering the life of the fetus, but it does not trump the rights of the mother, who retains full sovereignty over her body.

It is here that the expertise of the medical field becomes critical. No court, no judge, no politician can or should have a say in matters of life and death as they pertain to pregnancy and reproductive health. These decisions belong solely to those who are most educated and experienced in the complex realities of life and death—doctors. Physicians, having spent years training in the medical sciences, understanding the intricate balances between health, life, and risk, are the only ones equipped to make decisions about the viability of a fetus and the health of the mother.

Doctors take an oath to protect life, but they are also entrusted with the responsibility to protect the health and well-being of their patients. When a pregnancy endangers the life of the mother, it is the doctor's duty to prioritize her health while considering the life of the fetus, if viable. However, this decision can never be divorced from the consent and wishes of the mother. It is ultimately her body, her life, and her future at stake. Only she can make the final decision about what is best for her life, guided by the medical expertise of her doctor.

The idea that anyone other than a trained physician could overrule the decisions made in the operating room is a dangerous overreach. It not only undermines the professionalism of the medical field but places lives at risk. Politicians, judges, and lawmakers who do not understand the gravity of these life-and-death decisions should have no place in determining the outcome of a pregnancy. To do so is to disregard the sanctity of life itself, by placing bureaucratic ideology over medical science.

The law, while playing an essential role in regulating society, must respect the bounds of human rights and medical ethics. Any laws that attempt to take away the rights of a person to the usage of their own body, particularly in the context of pregnancy, are inherently flawed. These laws must always lean on the consensus of the medical field, which operates with the sole aim of protecting life, health, and human dignity.

Reasonable legal frameworks can exist that reflect the nuances of viability, health, and autonomy, but they must be rooted in the understanding that a person's right to bodily autonomy is sacrosanct. The law should protect a woman's right to choose, while relying on the expertise of the medical community to guide decisions on viability and health risks. At no point should the government override the judgment of doctors or the consent of the woman. To do so would be to reduce individuals to mere vessels, denying them their fundamental human rights.

In conclusion, no person, no institution, no law has the right to use another person's body without their consent. Just as we do not compel people to donate organs or blood against their will, we cannot compel a woman to carry a pregnancy to term if it endangers her life, health, or violates her autonomy. The decisions surrounding pregnancy and childbirth must remain with the person who inhabits the body and the doctors who have sworn to protect life. This is not just a matter of personal freedom—it is a matter of human dignity, respect, and ethical responsibility. Women are not vessels for forced reproduction; they are human beings with the right to make decisions about their own lives and futures.

Chapter 5: Indigenous and Historical Precedents for Equality

Long before the United States Constitution was drafted, indigenous societies across the Americas had already established sophisticated systems of governance that emphasized equality, individual sovereignty, and the balance of power between genders. Among these, the Iroquois Confederacy, also known as the Haudenosaunee, stands out for its *Great Law of Peace*, a foundational constitution that prioritized democratic decision-making and individual rights. This ancient law, created by the Five Nations of the Iroquois (later Six Nations with the addition of the Tuscarora), laid the groundwork for principles of governance that would later influence the American Founding Fathers.

In examining the Iroquois Confederacy's Great Law of Peace, as well as the broader roles of women in indigenous societies, we can uncover a powerful precedent for equality. Indigenous women were often treated as equals in ways that white American women were not. In fact, the stories of captive white women who preferred life with indigenous tribes to the oppressive gender norms of colonial American society illustrate the stark contrast between the relative freedom of indigenous societies and the restrictive confines of European settler culture. By exploring these historical precedents, we gain insight into how indigenous values of equality and sovereignty can inform and inspire modern activism for bodily autonomy and women's rights.

The Great Law of Peace and the Iroquois Confederacy

The Iroquois Confederacy's Great Law of Peace, which dates back to at least the 12th century, is one of the oldest and most sophisticated systems of governance in the world. The law brought together the Mohawk, Oneida, Onondaga, Cayuga, and Seneca nations into a united confederation. Later, the Tuscarora joined, making the Iroquois Confederacy a political entity that would last for centuries, well into the colonial period of North America.

At the core of the Great Law of Peace is the principle of collective decision-making through democratic means. The Confederacy was structured as a league of nations that maintained their sovereignty while agreeing to govern through consensus. This system relied on checks and balances, divided powers, and emphasized the importance of dialogue in resolving conflicts. The law codified principles of freedom and equality that were strikingly progressive for their time.

One of the most notable aspects of the Great Law of Peace was its inclusion of women in governance. In many indigenous societies, particularly within the Iroquois, women held significant power. They were responsible for selecting the male chiefs, known as *sachems*, who represented their clans in the Grand Council. These chiefs could be removed if they failed to serve the people, a power that women also held. Women had a say in political decisions, participated in the selection of leaders, and played vital roles in the social and economic life of their communities.

This matrilineal structure—where property and leadership roles were passed through the female line—ensured that women had a constant voice in the governance of the Confederacy. In contrast to the patriarchal structures of European settler society, where women were legally subordinate to men, indigenous women in the Iroquois Confederacy enjoyed a degree of autonomy and respect that was centuries ahead of its time.

Influence on the Founders

The Founding Fathers of the United States were deeply influenced by the political systems of indigenous nations, particularly the Iroquois Confederacy. Benjamin Franklin, in particular, admired the democratic nature of the Great Law of Peace and advocated for the inclusion of its principles in the formation of the American government. In 1751, Franklin wrote:

> "It would be a very strange thing if six Nations of ignorant savages should be capable of forming a scheme for such a Union… and yet that a like union should be impracticable for ten or a dozen English colonies." (Letter to James Parker, 1751)

Franklin and other Founders were impressed by the Confederacy's ability to maintain peace and cooperation among the Iroquois nations while preserving the sovereignty of each individual group. The Iroquois system of checks and balances, consensus-based decision-making, and respect for individual rights and responsibilities provided a model for the nascent United States as it sought to create its own democratic republic.

However, while the Founders drew inspiration from the Iroquois Confederacy, they did not fully adopt the inclusive values of the Great Law of Peace, particularly its treatment of women. The United States was founded on principles of liberty and equality, but these rights were explicitly reserved for white men. Women, along with enslaved people and indigenous populations, were excluded from the promises of freedom. In contrast, the Iroquois Confederacy recognized the importance of including women in governance and society—a lesson that modern movements for equality must continue to learn from.

The Role of Women in Indigenous Societies

Women in many indigenous societies, including the Iroquois, held far greater social, political, and economic power than their counterparts in European settler cultures. Indigenous women managed their own property, made key decisions about marriage and family life, and contributed to the survival and prosperity of their communities. Their roles were not limited to the domestic sphere; they were leaders, farmers, warriors, and spiritual guides.

In contrast, colonial American society treated women as legal dependents of their husbands or fathers. Women had few rights, no control over their own property, and were expected to submit to the authority of men in both public and private life. Marriage was often seen as a form of economic and social control, with women having little say in the major decisions that affected their lives.

This stark difference in gender roles became evident in the experiences of white women who were captured by indigenous tribes. Many of these women, once integrated into indigenous communities, found themselves enjoying greater freedoms than they had ever experienced in colonial society. They were treated as equals, valued for their contributions, and free from the restrictive gender norms that had previously governed their lives.

Captive Women and the Choice to Stay

One of the most compelling pieces of evidence for the relative freedom women enjoyed in indigenous societies comes from the testimonies of white women who were captured by Native American tribes and later chose to remain with their captors rather than return to colonial life. These women found a sense of autonomy and community within indigenous societies that was missing in the rigid, patriarchal structure of white settler culture.

For example, Mary Jemison, captured by the Seneca during the French and Indian War, chose to remain with the tribe for the rest of her life, even when given the opportunity to return to white society. In her memoir, Jemison described her new life with the Seneca as one of relative equality and contentment, compared to the harsher, more restricted life she had known among white settlers:

> "I was fully sensible that it was my duty to be contented in whatever situation I might be placed... and as my life was preserved, and the Indians treated me kindly, I concluded to make myself as happy as my situation would permit."

Other women, such as Cynthia Ann Parker, who was captured by the Comanche at the age of nine, also integrated fully into their new communities and resisted attempts by white society to "rescue" them. Parker, who married a Comanche chief and had children within the tribe, famously resisted her recapture by the Texas Rangers, and she spent the rest of her life longing to return to her Comanche family after being forcibly returned to white society.

These accounts are not isolated incidents. They reflect a broader pattern of women finding greater freedom, autonomy, and respect within indigenous societies compared to the oppressive and patriarchal norms of colonial America. For these women, the choice to remain with their indigenous communities was a rejection of the dominance and cruelty they had known in white society, where women were often treated as little more than property.

White Society's Oppression of Women and Children

The contrast between the treatment of women and children in indigenous and colonial societies is stark. White American society, particularly during the colonial and early national periods, was characterized by rigid gender hierarchies and the subjugation of women. Women were legally and socially subordinate to men, with few rights over their own bodies, property, or lives.

Children, too, were often subject to harsh discipline and strict control. In contrast, indigenous societies tended to treat children with greater compassion and allowed them more freedom to explore their environments and learn through experience. The cruelty of white society, with its rigid enforcement of gender roles and oppressive treatment of both women and children, stood in stark contrast to the relative freedom offered by indigenous communities.

These differences were so pronounced that many women, after experiencing life within indigenous societies, could not bear to return to the life of subservience they had once known. The stories of captive women who chose to stay with their indigenous families reveal the depth of oppression faced by women in white society, and they offer a powerful historical precedent for modern activism centered on bodily autonomy and gender equality.

Lessons from Indigenous Societies for Modern Activism

The history of the Iroquois Confederacy's Great Law of Peace and the broader role of women in indigenous societies offers a powerful counter-narrative to the patriarchal systems that have dominated much of Western history. The Iroquois Confederacy, with its emphasis on equality, individual sovereignty, and the inclusion of women in governance, provides a model for how societies can balance power and respect the autonomy of all individuals, regardless of gender.

The stories of captive women who chose to remain with indigenous tribes rather than return to white society further illustrate the profound difference in how women were treated. Indigenous societies offered them freedoms and respect that were denied in colonial America—a reminder that equality is not a new concept but one that has been practiced and valued by many cultures throughout history.

As we fight for bodily autonomy and gender equality today, we can draw inspiration from these historical precedents. Indigenous societies, particularly the Iroquois Confederacy, remind us that true equality is possible and that women can and should have a central role in shaping the future of our society. By reclaiming these values, we can build a movement that demands not only reproductive rights but full equality and sovereignty over our own bodies and lives.

Chapter 6: The Constitution and the Limitations of Freedom

The United States Constitution, often revered as a beacon of liberty and justice, remains a profoundly flawed document when it comes to addressing the rights of women. While it enshrines certain freedoms for a select group of citizens, it has utterly failed to guarantee the most basic right that should be afforded to all human beings—bodily autonomy. For women, this failure has been especially catastrophic, effectively relegating them to second-class status under a system that has long prioritized the rights of men.

The Constitution's silence on women's autonomy is not merely an oversight but a glaring injustice that has caused immense harm over the centuries. From the exclusion of women in political decision-making to their lack of control over reproductive health, the founding document of this country institutionalized a patriarchal system that continues to devalue and constrain half the population. The damage this has done is not just personal—it has stunted the progress of our civilization as a whole, removing the contributions of women from the intellectual and political landscape for generations.

It is time to recognize the fundamental wrongness of this failure and correct it, not just for the sake of justice but for the future of humanity.

The Constitution's Failure to Protect Women

The Founding Fathers are often hailed as visionaries, but in truth, they were deeply limited by the biases and cultural norms of their time. They crafted a document that protected the freedoms of white, land-owning men while failing to extend those same rights to women, enslaved people, and indigenous populations. Women were considered the property of their husbands and fathers, excluded from the rights to vote, own property independently, or exercise control over their own bodies.

The Constitution's failure to address women's rights was not an accident—it was an intentional omission. The Founders, influenced by centuries of patriarchal tradition and unscientific beliefs about gender, saw women as inherently inferior to men. They believed that women were too emotional, irrational, and weak to participate in the political sphere or to govern their own lives. This deeply ingrained gender bias became the foundation for laws that would, for centuries, deprive women of the most basic human rights.

The consequences of this exclusion have been devastating. By failing to recognize women's autonomy over their bodies, the Constitution effectively sanctioned their subjugation. For centuries, women were denied control over their reproductive choices, forced into marriages that they could not escape, and subjected to sexual and physical abuse without legal recourse. Women's bodies became battlegrounds for the enforcement of male control, with the government and society treating them as vessels for reproduction rather than autonomous individuals with inherent rights.

The Harm Done to Women by the Constitution's Failures

The most glaring harm caused by the Constitution's failure to address women's rights is the lack of bodily autonomy. For much of American history, women were denied the right to make decisions about their own reproductive health. Abortion was criminalized, birth control was restricted, and women were forced to carry pregnancies to term regardless of the risks to their health or well-being. Even today, with the overturning of *Roe v. Wade* in 2022, women in many states are once again losing the right to access safe and legal abortion, putting their lives in danger.

The failure to protect women's autonomy extends beyond reproductive rights. Women have historically been denied the ability to divorce abusive husbands, maintain custody of their children, or even escape sexual violence. Marital rape was not considered a crime in most states until the 1970s, and in many cases, women were legally bound to remain in marriages with men who abused them physically, sexually, and emotionally. The legal system's failure to protect women from violence is a direct result of the Constitution's silence on women's rights.

This institutionalized oppression has had long-term effects on women's economic independence, health, and psychological well-being. Without control over their own bodies, women have been unable to fully participate in the workforce, pursue education, or engage in public life. The notion that women are inherently suited for domesticity and motherhood has been used to justify their exclusion from political, economic, and intellectual spheres, robbing society of their potential contributions.

The Founding Fathers' Mistakes and Their Legacy

The Founding Fathers, while celebrated for their contributions to democracy, were deeply flawed men who failed to envision a society where women could be equals. Their decision to exclude women from the Constitution was rooted in misogyny, supported by unscientific ideas about gender that depicted women as inferior to men. They borrowed these ideas from centuries of European patriarchy, reinforced by religious doctrines that promoted the subjugation of women.

By refusing to acknowledge women's equality, the Founders essentially enslaved half the population to the other half. Women were denied the right to vote until 1920, over a century after the Constitution was written, and even then, their rights were heavily restricted by gender norms that limited their access to political and economic power. The Founders' decision to codify male dominance into the legal framework of the nation has caused lasting damage, perpetuating cycles of poverty, violence, and discrimination against women.

The long-term consequences of this exclusion are staggering. By silencing women's voices and denying them the ability to fully participate in society, the Founding Fathers limited the intellectual and creative potential of the nation.

How many scientific discoveries, political reforms, and technological innovations were lost because women were denied the opportunity to contribute?   How much human progress has been hampered by the fact that half the population was excluded from the conversation?

The oppression of women has not only been a moral failing—it has also been a practical one. By shutting out women's ideas, leadership, and innovation, the Founders handicapped the development of American society. Imagine the world we could live in today if women had been granted full rights from the beginning. If women had been free to contribute to science, politics, art, and technology on an equal footing with men, we might already be exploring the stars. Instead, our civilization has been held back by centuries of inequality.

The Benefits of a Society of Equals

The idea that society would benefit from gender equality is not speculative—it is supported by centuries of evidence. Societies that value and empower women are more prosperous, more peaceful, and more innovative. When women have the freedom to contribute their ideas and labor on an equal footing with men, the entire nation benefits.

In countries where women's rights have been advanced, we see higher levels of economic growth, better health outcomes, and more stable political systems. Women bring diverse perspectives and approaches to problem-solving, and their inclusion in decision-making leads to more comprehensive and equitable policies. In business, companies with women in leadership positions consistently outperform those that lack gender diversity. In politics, nations with women in government tend to have more inclusive policies that benefit a wider range of citizens.

Bodily autonomy is central to achieving these benefits. When women have control over their own reproductive health, they are better able to plan their families, pursue education, and participate in the workforce. The freedom to make decisions about their own bodies allows women to contribute fully to society, rather than being constrained by the demands of motherhood or forced pregnancies. Countries that ensure women's reproductive rights are more prosperous and better equipped to handle the challenges of modern life.

Moreover, gender equality fosters a culture of innovation. Societies that value all citizens equally create the conditions for intellectual and creative breakthroughs. When all people are free to contribute their ideas and talents, regardless of gender, humanity moves forward. The inclusion of women in science, technology, and the arts has already led to incredible advancements, from medical breakthroughs to new forms of artistic expression.

Correcting Course and Propelling Civilization Forward

Correcting the mistakes of the Founding Fathers is not just about righting historical wrongs—it is about unlocking the full potential of human civilization. By granting women full bodily autonomy and enshrining their rights in the Constitution, we can create a society where everyone is free to contribute to the betterment of humanity. A society of equals is one that is better equipped to solve the problems of the future, from climate change to space exploration.

Imagine what we could achieve if every person, regardless of gender, was free to pursue their passions and ideas. With the full intellectual and creative power of humanity unleashed, we could make rapid advancements in science, technology, and politics. Women, who have historically been sidelined, could bring fresh perspectives and solutions to the world's most pressing challenges.   We could move beyond the limitations of patriarchal thinking and create a future where progress is driven by collaboration, creativity, and equality.

The fight for bodily autonomy is not just a women's issue—it is a human issue. It is about creating a world where every person is valued for their contributions, where no one is held back by outdated and oppressive systems. By correcting the course set by the Founders, we can propel our civilization into the future, moving beyond the constraints of inequality and into an era of true progress.

A Future of Equals

The U.S. Constitution, as it stands, is an incomplete promise of freedom. It has failed to protect women's bodily autonomy, and in doing so, it has failed to protect the fundamental rights of half the population. The time has come to correct this injustice and recognize that true freedom requires the inclusion of all people, regardless of gender. The progress of civilization depends on it.

71

By ensuring women's full bodily autonomy and enshrining it in law, we can create a society of equals—one that values every person's contributions and unleashes the full potential of humanity. The future we envision is one where women are no longer constrained by the limitations imposed by a patriarchal system, but are free to innovate, lead, and explore. This future is within our reach, but it requires bold action and a willingness to correct the course set by history.

The Constitution's failure to address women's rights has caused immense harm, but by correcting that failure, we can build a better world for future generations. A society of equals is not just a possibility—it is a necessity for the continued advancement of humanity. It is time to demand the freedom that was promised, not just for men, but for all people.

Chapter 7: A Call for an Amendment Guaranteeing the Inviolability of Personal Sovereignty Over One's Body

At the heart of the American identity lies a deep belief in freedom, self-determination, and justice. From the fight for independence to the battles for civil rights, Americans have always strived to create a society where each individual's autonomy and liberty are respected and protected. Yet, despite this storied history, there remains a glaring omission in the nation's legal framework: the failure to guarantee the inviolability of personal sovereignty over one's body. It is time to correct this omission by enacting a constitutional amendment that affirms every individual's right to bodily autonomy.

This amendment is not just about protecting women's reproductive rights, though that is central to it. It is about the fundamental belief that no person should be subjected to the control of another, whether by the state, a partner, or an institution. It is about recognizing that the body is sacred, and the decisions about it belong solely to the individual. This ideal—of liberty, autonomy, and self-governance—defines what it means to be American. As Dr. Martin Luther King Jr. once said, "Injustice anywhere is a threat to justice everywhere," and the ongoing injustice of denying bodily autonomy must be addressed for the sake of justice everywhere in our nation.

The Suffragette Movement: A Fight for Equality

The fight for women's right to vote in the early 20th century offers a powerful precedent for this new call for personal sovereignty. Suffragettes, the brave women who fought for the right to vote, faced unimaginable challenges in their quest for equality. They endured public slander, police brutality, and imprisonment, but they remained resolute in their belief that women deserved the same political rights as men. This fight was about more than just voting—it was about women's inherent dignity and their right to participate fully in society.

Many suffragettes were vilified in the media, portrayed as irrational, hysterical, or unfeminine. The national press, heavily dominated by male voices, sought to discredit their movement by focusing on their supposed "unladylike" behavior, attempting to sow fear among the public that granting women the right to vote would destroy the fabric of American society. But these attacks only strengthened their resolve.

Women like **Alice Paul**, **Lucy Burns**, and **Ida B. Wells** led marches, organized protests, and demanded their rights, despite the constant threat of violence. Suffragettes were jailed for picketing outside the White House. The infamous "Night of Terror" in 1917 saw suffragettes beaten, thrown into cold cells, and denied basic human rights at the Occoquan Workhouse in Virginia. Women were force-fed after going on hunger strikes, a brutal and dehumanizing practice that further exposed the inhumanity of those who sought to suppress their voices.

Some women even lost their lives in the struggle for suffrage. **Inez Milholland**, one of the most prominent suffragettes and an inspiring public speaker, died in 1916 while on a national speaking tour for women's rights. Her last public words, "Mr. President, how long must women wait for liberty?" have become a rallying cry for generations of women fighting for equality.

Despite these horrors, the suffragette movement persisted. Women across the country fought back against the media's slander and the violence of law enforcement with unwavering determination. Suffragettes demonstrated an unparalleled strength of will, knowing that their fight was for the future of all women. Eventually, many men joined their cause, recognizing the injustice of denying women the vote. The political landscape shifted, and by 1920, the 19th Amendment was passed, granting women the right to vote and transforming American society forever.

The Impact of the Suffrage Movement on Society

The passage of the 19th Amendment not only changed the political landscape but also had profound effects on American life. For women, the right to vote symbolized their full entry into public life. It empowered them to influence policies that affected their families, communities, and country. But the impact of the suffrage movement extended far beyond women—it benefited society as a whole, including men.

Before the 19th Amendment, American life was steeped in rigid gender roles. Women were expected to stay at home, tending to domestic tasks, while men governed the political and economic spheres. This divide limited not only women's potential but also the overall progress of society. By excluding half the population from contributing to the nation's decision-making, America effectively cut off half its potential for innovation, growth, and improvement.

Once women gained the right to vote, they began to shape the nation in ways that benefitted everyone. Women played a pivotal role in advocating for social reforms such as labor laws, child welfare, and public health initiatives. Their voices helped push for workplace safety regulations, food safety standards, and education reform—issues that affected all Americans, not just women. Women's suffrage helped push America toward becoming a more compassionate and just society.

Moreover, granting women the vote created a more balanced and representative democracy. As women's rights expanded, men's lives improved as well. The family unit became more egalitarian, with men sharing in domestic responsibilities and women having greater economic opportunities. Societal progress in areas like healthcare, education, and economic equality accelerated as women gained greater political and social influence.

A more inclusive society benefits everyone, and the fight for suffrage proved this beyond any doubt. The struggle and eventual victory of the suffragette movement transformed America, demonstrating that expanding rights and recognizing equality creates a stronger, more just nation. The gains made by women uplifted everyone, providing further evidence that the fight for women's equality is a fight for the betterment of society as a whole.

The Need for a New Amendment: Bodily Autonomy

Just as the 19th Amendment transformed the political landscape by recognizing women's right to vote, a new amendment enshrining bodily autonomy would profoundly reshape American society for the better. The right to control one's own body is the most basic human right, and yet, for too long, women have been denied this fundamental freedom. It is time for the Constitution to reflect the reality that every individual has the right to make decisions about their own body without interference from the government, religious institutions, or any other external force.

The women who fought for suffrage knew that their battle was not just about the vote—it was about their right to be recognized as full and equal human beings. Today, the fight for bodily autonomy is no different. Women's bodies have been controlled and regulated for centuries, from reproductive rights to medical decisions, and it is time to end this injustice once and for all.

A constitutional amendment guaranteeing the inviolability of personal sovereignty over one's body would not only protect reproductive rights but also establish a precedent for greater individual freedom. This amendment would ensure that no one could be forced to undergo medical procedures, including childbirth, against their will. It would guarantee the right to privacy and bodily integrity, making it clear that every person has the exclusive right to decide what happens to their body.

The argument for bodily autonomy is not just about women—it is about all people. The benefits of this amendment would extend to men, children, and marginalized communities. Just as the 19th Amendment uplifted the entire nation, an amendment for bodily autonomy would create a more just and equitable society for everyone.

Overcoming the Challenges

Just as the suffragettes faced violent opposition and media slander, the fight for bodily autonomy will encounter fierce resistance. Already, we see how reproductive rights are under attack, with politicians, religious leaders, and the media attempting to control the narrative and paint those advocating for bodily autonomy as radical or immoral. But history shows us that when justice is on the side of the people, progress cannot be stopped.

The suffragette movement provides a blueprint for how to fight—and win—this battle. It took decades of organizing, protesting, and educating the public before women gained the right to vote, and the same will be true for the fight for bodily autonomy. But just as the suffragettes eventually triumphed, so too can we achieve a victory for personal sovereignty.

Men, too, will play a crucial role in this fight, just as they did in the suffrage movement. As more men recognize that bodily autonomy is a fundamental human right, they will join the fight, just as they did for women's right to vote.

When men and women come together to demand justice, they create an unstoppable force for change.

A Future of True Freedom

The time has come for America to live up to its ideals. The principles of liberty, justice, and self-determination must extend to every person, and that means enshrining the inviolability of personal sovereignty over one's body in the Constitution. Just as the suffragettes fought for the right to vote, we must now fight for the right to control our own bodies.

The 19th Amendment transformed America, paving the way for social progress and equality that benefited not just women but the entire nation. A new amendment for bodily autonomy would do the same, ensuring that every person, regardless of gender, has the freedom to make decisions about their own body. It would create a more just society, one in which everyone has the right to self-governance and personal freedom.

This is the next great battle for civil rights, and like the suffragettes, we will not be silenced. It is time to rise up and demand the justice that has been denied to us for too long. With an amendment for bodily autonomy, we will create a future of true freedom—freedom for women, for men, for everyone. The fight begins now.

Chapter 8: Medical Evidence and the Consequences of Government Interference

As the wave of abortion bans and restrictive reproductive health laws sweeps across the United States, the medical community is witnessing firsthand the devastating consequences of these policies. The harm caused by government interference in reproductive health care is mounting, and the data—though still emerging—paints a grim picture. Lives are being lost, physical and psychological suffering is intensifying, and families are being torn apart as the legal landscape surrounding reproductive rights becomes more restrictive.

In states like Texas and Georgia, where some of the most draconian abortion laws have been implemented, reports of women dying as a result of these laws are now coming to light. These tragedies are just the beginning, as the full scale of the damage wrought by these laws will only become clearer in the coming years. Furthermore, innocent women who have suffered miscarriages are being subjected to legal scrutiny and criminal charges, further exacerbating the trauma they endure. We will examine the medical evidence, case studies, and testimonies from doctors to demonstrate the profound harm that government interference in reproductive health care is inflicting on women and children across the country.

The recent wave of restrictive laws surrounding reproductive healthcare in the United States, especially those targeting abortion access, has created a healthcare crisis of tragic proportions. With states like Texas and Georgia leading the charge, the rollback of abortion rights following the 2022 *Dobbs v. Jackson* decision has exposed women to heightened risks of physical, psychological, and social harm. While the full scope of this damage is only beginning to emerge, the early data paint a harrowing picture of the consequences. These restrictions do not only affect women seeking abortions; they ripple through the entire healthcare system, putting all pregnant individuals at risk and compromising the safety of even those who suffer miscarriages.

Delve into the growing body of medical evidence that demonstrates the harm caused by government interference in reproductive healthcare. We will examine the impact of abortion bans on maternal mortality rates, healthcare access, mental health, and the well-being of children born into untenable circumstances. We will also present testimonies from healthcare providers and case studies from women who have been directly harmed by these restrictive laws.

The Emerging Data: A Crisis Unfolding

The reversal of *Roe v. Wade* in 2022 unleashed a wave of restrictive abortion laws in states across the country, leading to a patchwork of reproductive rights that varies drastically depending on where a woman lives. In states like Texas, Georgia, and Alabama, laws have been enacted that severely limit or outright ban access to abortion, even in cases of rape, incest, or when the life of the mother is at risk. These laws have forced medical providers into difficult, and often dangerous, positions—resulting in delayed care, inadequate treatment, and an overall decline in maternal health outcomes.

One of the most concerning effects of these laws is the rising maternal mortality rate. In Texas, for example, data from the Texas Maternal Mortality and Morbidity Review Committee shows that the state already had one of the highest maternal mortality rates in the developed world, even before its abortion restrictions were put into place. In 2018, Texas reported 18.5 maternal deaths per 100,000 live births, a figure significantly higher than other developed countries. Since the implementation of the state's restrictive abortion law, reports of maternal deaths are on the rise, though full statistics are still being gathered.

Physicians in states with restrictive abortion laws report an alarming increase in cases where women are denied life-saving medical care due to legal uncertainty. In several states, medical providers are required to wait until a woman is on the brink of death before intervening in pregnancy-related complications. This hesitation, driven by fear of legal consequences, has led to delays in treatment for conditions such as ectopic pregnancies, severe infections, and other life-threatening complications. Women who could have been saved with timely medical intervention are instead left to suffer, and in some cases, die.

One recent case involved a woman in Texas who was forced to wait for her life-threatening ectopic pregnancy to rupture before doctors could legally intervene. By the time she was treated, the delay had caused irreversible damage to her health, and her case is just one of many. Doctors across the country are expressing outrage and frustration as they are forced to navigate a legal landscape that prioritizes political ideology over patient safety.

The Psychological Toll on Women

The physical harms caused by abortion restrictions are accompanied by profound psychological trauma. Studies show that women who are denied access to abortion face higher rates of mental health issues, including depression, anxiety, and post-traumatic stress disorder. The **Turnaway Study**, a landmark research project conducted by the University of California, San Francisco, followed women who sought abortions but were turned away due to gestational limits. The study found that women who were denied abortions were more likely to experience long-term psychological distress, including anxiety and depression, compared to women who received the care they needed.

Moreover, the criminalization of miscarriages and stillbirths has added a new layer of trauma for women. In several states, women who experience pregnancy loss are being investigated for potential wrongdoing, often enduring invasive legal inquiries into their personal lives. In Georgia, one woman was charged with second-degree murder after suffering a miscarriage at 5 months, accused of "self-managing" her abortion, despite no evidence supporting the claim. This kind of legal harassment compounds the grief and trauma of losing a pregnancy, leaving women feeling isolated, criminalized, and victimized by a system that should be supporting them.

The Suffering of Children Born Into Untenable Circumstances

The consequences of abortion restrictions extend beyond the immediate harm to women—they also profoundly affect the lives of children born into circumstances that are untenable. Forcing women to carry unwanted pregnancies to term leads to children being born into situations where they may face neglect, poverty, and inadequate care. According to a study published by the Guttmacher Institute, approximately 75% of women who seek abortions in the U.S. are living at or below the federal poverty line. Denying these women access to reproductive care only exacerbates the cycle of poverty, as they are forced to raise children without the necessary financial resources.

These children often grow up in environments where they lack access to adequate nutrition, healthcare, and education. The American Academy of Pediatrics has long warned that children born into poverty are more likely to experience developmental delays, chronic illnesses, and poor educational outcomes. Furthermore, these children are more likely to suffer from mental health issues and to experience abuse or neglect in households that are overwhelmed and under-resourced.

Testimonies from Medical Professionals

Doctors on the front lines of reproductive healthcare are speaking out about the harm caused by these restrictive laws. Dr. Jamila Perritt, an OB-GYN and the president of Physicians for Reproductive Health, has witnessed firsthand

the devastating impact these laws are having on women's
health:

> "We are seeing patients in distress, and we are
> unable to provide them the care they need
> because we are hamstrung by laws that do not
> prioritize patient safety. Every day, women's lives
> are being put at risk because of political
> interference in medical care."

Another OB-GYN from Texas, who wished to remain
anonymous due to fear of legal repercussions, shared a
heartbreaking case where a woman with sepsis caused by an
incomplete miscarriage was left waiting for hours as doctors
sought legal clarity on whether they could intervene. By the
time treatment was administered, the woman's condition had
deteriorated so badly that she had to undergo a hysterectomy
to save her life, leaving her permanently unable to have
children.

Case Studies of Women Harmed by Government Interference

In addition to the rising maternal mortality rate,
numerous individual cases highlight the very real human toll
these laws are taking. A woman in Georgia, *Samantha*,
experienced a miscarriage at 16 weeks but was denied a
dilation and curettage (D&C), a procedure used to remove
fetal tissue, because hospital staff feared repercussions under
the state's new abortion law. She was sent home and endured
severe physical pain, bleeding, and emotional trauma over the
course of several days before the hospital finally intervened.
Her story mirrors countless others—women left to suffer

unnecessarily because medical professionals are unsure of their legal standing.

In another case from Ohio, *Tara*, a mother of two, was diagnosed with a life-threatening condition called preeclampsia during her pregnancy. Her doctors advised her to terminate the pregnancy, but the state's restrictive laws made it impossible for her to access an abortion. Tara was forced to continue the pregnancy, risking her own life in the process. By the time she reached 24 weeks, her condition had worsened so dramatically that doctors were left with no choice but to induce labor, resulting in the premature birth and death of her child. Tara was left physically weakened and emotionally devastated, her health permanently damaged by a law that placed ideology over medical necessity.

The Long-Term Consequences of Government Interference

The long-term consequences of government interference in reproductive health are staggering. Women's health is deteriorating as access to safe and timely medical care becomes increasingly restricted. The maternal mortality rate in states with strict abortion bans is expected to rise sharply, compounding an already alarming trend in a country that is supposed to lead the world in healthcare.

Furthermore, the psychological trauma inflicted on women who are forced to carry unwanted pregnancies, face criminal charges for miscarriages, or endure life-threatening conditions without medical intervention will have lasting effects on the mental health of the population. Children born into poverty and neglect, as a result of these laws, will also suffer, perpetuating cycles of poverty and inequality that will reverberate for generations.

The Consequences of Abortion Bans: The Medical Data

The decision to restrict or outright ban abortion has resulted in a healthcare catastrophe, particularly in states where the laws are most stringent. As of 2023, 14 states have implemented near-total bans on abortion, and many others have enacted restrictions that severely limit access to reproductive healthcare. The consequences of these laws are just now coming to light, and the data already show that the impact is far worse than many experts anticipated.

The most immediate and alarming consequence of these restrictions is the sharp rise in maternal mortality rates. The United States already had one of the highest maternal mortality rates in the developed world before the reversal of *Roe v. Wade*. Now, in states with restrictive abortion laws, the situation has become even more dire.

A 2022 study from the *Commonwealth Fund* found that maternal mortality rates are significantly higher in states with abortion restrictions compared to states with more permissive laws. The maternal mortality rate in the United States overall was 23.8 deaths per 100,000 live births in 2020, but in states like Texas and Georgia, where abortion laws have become increasingly restrictive, that number has surged to over 40 deaths per 100,000 live births . This rise is attributed to several factors, including reduced access to reproductive healthcare, delayed care, and the forced continuation of high-risk pregnancies.

In Georgia, one of the first states to implement a six-week abortion ban, maternal deaths have increased by over 20% since the law went into effect . Doctors report that women with life-threatening pregnancy complications, such as ectopic pregnancies and severe preeclampsia, are now being denied timely medical interventions for fear of legal repercussions. This delay in care has resulted in preventable deaths, as healthcare providers are forced to prioritize legal concerns over patient well-being.

In Texas, where the "Heartbeat Bill" has outlawed abortion after six weeks, maternal mortality rates are also climbing. A 2023 report by *The New England Journal of Medicine* found that women in Texas are now 25% more likely to die during childbirth than before the law was enacted . The state's strict abortion ban has created a climate of fear among healthcare providers, leading to dangerous delays in treating pregnancy complications. Women with incomplete miscarriages, for instance, are often forced to wait until they are on the brink of sepsis before doctors feel legally safe to intervene.

Mental Health and Psychological Trauma

In addition to the physical risks, the psychological toll of forced pregnancies and restricted reproductive healthcare cannot be overstated. Numerous studies have demonstrated the connection between access to abortion and mental health outcomes. When women are denied abortions, they are more likely to experience long-term mental health issues, including depression, anxiety, and post-traumatic stress disorder (PTSD).

A landmark study known as "The Turnaway Study," conducted by researchers at the *University of California, San Francisco* and published in 2020, tracked the mental health outcomes of women who were denied abortions compared to those who were able to access the procedure. The study found that women who were denied abortions were significantly more likely to experience long-term psychological distress. They reported higher rates of depression, anxiety, and suicidal thoughts, as well as lower self-esteem and life satisfaction .

The psychological effects are particularly severe for women who are forced to carry pregnancies resulting from rape or incest. In states like Alabama and Missouri, where abortion is banned with no exceptions for rape or incest, survivors of sexual violence are forced to endure the trauma of pregnancy and childbirth against their will. The mental health consequences of such forced pregnancies are profound, leading to increased rates of PTSD and suicidal ideation.

In Texas, several women who were denied abortions after suffering severe fetal abnormalities have spoken out about the psychological torture of being forced to continue pregnancies they knew would end in the death of their child. One woman, Marlena Stell, shared her harrowing story of being denied an abortion after her fetus was diagnosed with anencephaly, a fatal condition in which the baby is born without parts of the brain and skull. Despite knowing that her baby would not survive, Stell was forced to carry the pregnancy to term, enduring months of emotional anguish and physical pain.

Case Studies: Women Harmed by Government Interference

The human cost of these laws can be seen in the stories of women who have suffered under the weight of restrictive abortion policies. Their experiences highlight the brutal consequences of government interference in personal healthcare decisions.

Case Study 1: Amanda Zurawski, Texas

Amanda Zurawski, a 34-year-old woman from Texas, was 18 weeks pregnant when she learned that her baby was no longer viable. Under normal circumstances, she would have been offered an abortion to protect her health, but due to Texas's abortion ban, her doctors told her they could not intervene until she showed signs of infection. Days later, Zurawski developed sepsis and was rushed to the hospital, where she nearly died from the delay in care. She later said, "The doctors knew that I needed an abortion, but their hands were tied by the law. I came within hours of losing my life because politicians made my medical decisions for me" .

Case Study 2: Savita Halappanavar, Ireland (A Warning for the U.S.)

Though not a U.S. case, the tragic death of Savita Halappanavar in Ireland in 2012 serves as a warning of what can happen when abortion is restricted. Halappanavar, a 31-year-old dentist, was 17 weeks pregnant when she began to miscarry. Despite knowing the pregnancy was nonviable, doctors refused to perform an abortion due to Ireland's strict anti-abortion laws. Halappanavar died from septic shock after days of agony. Her death sparked widespread protests and eventually led to the repeal of Ireland's abortion ban. Her case is a stark reminder of the dangers of delaying care due to restrictive laws .

The Suffering of Children Born into Untenable Circumstances

The consequences of abortion restrictions extend beyond the women forced to carry unwanted or dangerous pregnancies. Children born into untenable circumstances—whether due to poverty, abuse, or severe medical conditions—suffer as well. Many of these children are born into families that lack the resources to care for them, leading to poor health outcomes, developmental delays, and higher rates of abuse and neglect.

A study conducted by the *Guttmacher Institute* found that nearly 75% of women who seek abortions cite financial instability as a primary reason for not being able to continue their pregnancies. When these women are denied abortions, they are forced to raise children in environments where their basic needs cannot be met . The children born into these circumstances often suffer the consequences of poverty, lack of access to healthcare, and unstable living conditions.

Furthermore, children born with severe medical conditions are often subjected to prolonged suffering. In states where abortion is banned even in cases of fetal abnormalities, women are forced to carry pregnancies to term, only for their children to die shortly after birth. These children endure short lives filled with pain and suffering—lives that could have been mercifully ended before birth, sparing both the child and the family further trauma.

91

The Healthcare Provider's Dilemma

Healthcare providers, especially those in states with restrictive abortion laws, are placed in an untenable position. They are forced to navigate complex legal frameworks while trying to provide the best care for their patients. Many doctors report feeling trapped between their medical ethics, which compel them to prioritize patient safety, and the legal restrictions that could land them in jail if they perform abortions under certain circumstances.

Dr. Jennifer Kerns, an OB-GYN and abortion provider, described the chilling effect of these laws:

> "Doctors are terrified. We're afraid that any action we take to save a woman's life could be interpreted as an illegal abortion. So, we wait. We wait until the woman's life is truly at risk, and by then, it's often too late" .

Doctors have also spoken out about the emotional toll of being unable to offer the care their patients need. Many report feeling helpless as they watch women suffer needlessly due to the legal constraints imposed by their states. One physician in Georgia recounted the story of a young woman with an ectopic pregnancy who was denied treatment for hours because hospital lawyers needed to ensure they would not be violating the state's abortion ban. By the time she received care, her fallopian tube had ruptured, causing significant internal bleeding .

The Unfolding Tragedy

The harm caused by government interference in reproductive healthcare is already devastating, and the full scope of this crisis is only just beginning to come to light. The data and personal stories from states like Texas and Georgia provide a glimpse into the profound physical, psychological, and emotional damage these laws are inflicting on women. Maternal mortality rates are climbing, mental health issues are worsening, and healthcare providers are trapped in a legal limbo that forces them to delay or deny care to women in desperate need.

The consequences are not limited to the immediate health of women—they extend to the children born into circumstances of poverty, illness, or familial instability, where they suffer greatly due to a lack of resources and care. Women who are forced to carry unwanted or nonviable pregnancies to term are left to endure a nightmare of trauma and grief, with long-lasting effects on their mental and physical health.

These abortion bans are not just a legal issue—they represent a profound moral and human rights crisis. Women are being denied the basic right to make decisions about their own bodies, and the cost of this denial is measured in lives lost, families shattered, and futures stolen. As we gather more data in the years to come, it will become even clearer that these laws have inflicted a devastating toll on countless women and children.

To correct this tragedy, it is imperative that we advocate for laws and constitutional protections that guarantee every person the right to bodily autonomy. As the medical evidence shows, when women are denied control over their own bodies, they suffer—and so does society as a whole. The time for change is now, and the fight for bodily autonomy must continue until every woman has the freedom to make the decisions that affect her health, her life, and her future.

Chapter 9: We Don't Have Time to Be Nice About This

America is teetering on the brink of a socio-economic disaster. The inequality baked into the system, reinforced by outdated gender roles, religious dogma, and oppressive policies, is actively destroying the American family. Inequality doesn't just damage women's autonomy; it erodes the very foundation of society, driving families into dysfunction, economic ruin, and despair. We are witnessing the collapse of a system that no longer supports its people, and the consequences will be catastrophic unless drastic changes are made.

The forced birth agenda, coupled with the push to roll back no-fault divorce laws, is not about strengthening families. It is about entrenching power dynamics that treat women as subservient and men as entitled masters of the household. This archaic worldview is fueling abusive family structures, increasing divorce rates, and creating an unsustainable economic burden on American families. In short, inequality and religious dogma are killing the American dream.

At the same time, the economic reality of modern America is grim: two-parent households can no longer make ends meet on their incomes, the housing market has become an unattainable goal for millions, and private equity firms are driving housing prices sky-high. The very notion of bringing children into this environment is not only unreasonable—it's cruel. The system is broken, and the vision of America's future is one of a dystopian nightmare where millions of families are left homeless and destitute.

The Destructive Effects of Inequality on the Family

Inequality has long been sold as a necessary part of the family structure, with men positioned as breadwinners and women as domestic caretakers. But this model, rooted in a toxic combination of entitlement and control, has only led to widespread unhappiness, broken families, and abuse. Forcing women into subservient roles not only harms them but also destabilizes the entire family unit.

One of the most significant drivers of divorce in America is the unequal division of labor in households. A 2021 study from the *American Sociological Association* found that women in heterosexual relationships are still overwhelmingly responsible for domestic chores, even when both partners work full-time. This imbalance fosters resentment and dissatisfaction, contributing to the rising divorce rate. Men, conditioned to see their wives as docile, unpaid servants, often react with frustration or aggression when confronted with the reality of shared responsibility.

This gendered inequality also breeds abuse. Men who feel entitled to control over women, emotionally and physically, are more likely to become abusive when they perceive that control slipping. Domestic violence in America is a tragic epidemic: according to the *National Coalition Against Domestic Violence*, nearly 1 in 4 women experience severe intimate partner physical violence, and the majority of these cases occur within households steeped in traditional, patriarchal values.

But it's not just women who suffer. Children raised in abusive or unequal households are more likely to exhibit behavioral problems, struggle in school, and face mental health challenges later in life. These children are also more likely to become abusers or victims of abuse themselves, perpetuating a cycle of violence that tears apart families generation after generation.

As more women demand equality within relationships —whether through shared household duties, reproductive rights, or the freedom to pursue careers—the backlash from men who feel entitled to traditional gender roles has become a primary driver of family instability. The patriarchal vision of the family, which forces women into a role of submission and demands that men be the sole authority, is incompatible with the realities of modern life. Clinging to this model ensures that families will continue to fracture.

The Economic Nightmare: Families Can't Survive on Two Incomes Anymore

It's not just interpersonal inequality that's breaking families—it's economic inequality, too. The economic conditions for families in the United States have deteriorated to the point where even dual-income households can barely make ends meet. The cost of living has skyrocketed, but wages have stagnated, leaving families trapped in a cycle of debt, financial insecurity, and despair.

Consider the situation in **San Francisco**, where the median home price is now over $1.4 million. According to the *National Association of Realtors*, only 15% of San Francisco residents can afford to buy a home. The cost of living in this city is so astronomical that even households with two adults earning six-figure salaries struggle to afford the basics—housing, healthcare, and education. In **New York City**, the situation is similarly dire: the median rent for a one-bedroom apartment is over $3,000 a month, while the average household income in the city remains just above $68,000. The disparity between wages and the cost of living is making it impossible for many families to survive without multiple sources of income.

This housing crisis is not limited to coastal cities. Across the United States, the housing market is increasingly controlled by **private equity firms** and **corporate landlords** who are driving up home prices and rent. Companies like **Blackstone** and **Invitation Homes** have bought up vast swaths of housing stock, turning once-affordable homes into expensive rental properties. As a result, homeownership—a traditional cornerstone of family stability—has become an unattainable dream for millions of Americans.

A recent study by the *Joint Center for Housing Studies* at Harvard University found that nearly 40 million households in the U.S. are now considered "housing cost burdened," meaning they spend more than 30% of their income on housing. Over 18 million of these households are spending more than half of their income on rent or mortgages, leaving little left for food, healthcare, education, or saving for the future.

The Dystopian Future: Homeless Families and Societal Collapse

What happens when families can no longer afford housing, healthcare, or basic necessities? The answer is dystopian: millions of families are on the brink of financial collapse, and if current trends continue, America will soon face a housing crisis of unprecedented proportions. We are already seeing the early signs of this disaster. Homelessness is rising across the country, with tent cities popping up in major metropolitan areas like Los Angeles, Seattle, and San Francisco. According to the *U.S. Department of Housing and Urban Development*, more than half a million people experience homelessness on any given night in America, and that number is expected to rise as housing becomes increasingly unaffordable.

Imagine a future where millions of American families are living out of their cars, unable to afford rent or buy homes, forced into ghettos or sprawling homeless encampments. This isn't a hypothetical scenario—it's the future we are headed toward if the current trends of inequality and economic mismanagement continue. The combination of forced birth policies, low wages, skyrocketing housing costs, and the rollback of women's rights will create a society where the American dream is completely out of reach for the majority of the population.

This is the dystopian future: a society where families are crammed into slums, barely surviving, while a small elite class walls themselves off in gated communities of extreme wealth and decadence. This is the path the United States is on unless we make radical changes to the way we treat women, families, and economic inequality.

The Religious Dogma and Forced Birth Agenda Will Make This Worse

Rather than addressing these growing inequalities and the fragility of the American family, the right-wing agenda is to double down on policies that will make the situation even worse. The forced birth agenda, which seeks to deny women reproductive rights, coupled with efforts to overturn no-fault divorce laws, will further entrench inequality and create even more dysfunctional family structures.

Forcing women to carry pregnancies to term in an environment where they cannot financially or emotionally support a child is a recipe for disaster. As we've seen in countries that restrict reproductive rights, such policies lead to higher rates of poverty, child abuse, and domestic violence. Children born into families that cannot support them face immense challenges, from malnutrition to poor educational outcomes. These children often become trapped in cycles of poverty that they are unable to escape.

The religious dogma that drives the forced birth agenda ignores these realities, insisting that women's primary purpose is to bear children regardless of their circumstances. But in an economy where families can no longer afford housing or healthcare, where the average American can no longer buy a home, this approach is not only outdated—it's actively harmful. The result will be an America where millions of unwanted children are born into families that cannot support them, creating a generation of poverty, desperation, and social instability.

America's Uncertain Future: A Warning

If we continue down this path, America's future will look increasingly like India's: a nation with vast inequalities, where the majority of the population lives in poverty while a tiny elite hoards the wealth. In India, millions of people live in slums with little access to healthcare, education, or clean water, while the country's wealthiest individuals live in sprawling estates walled off from the suffering of the masses. This is the future America is heading toward if we do not address the rampant inequality, the forced birth agenda, and the housing crisis.

The middle class is shrinking, and more Americans are falling into poverty. As housing becomes increasingly unaffordable and wages fail to keep up with the cost of living, the American dream will become a distant memory for most. Families will struggle to survive, and the social fabric of the country will unravel. The forced birth agenda, far from saving families, will hasten this collapse by forcing women into economic and social conditions they cannot escape.

Time to Act

We don't have time to be polite about this anymore. Inequality, forced birth, and economic collapse are destroying the American family. The combination of religious dogma, outdated gender roles, and skyrocketing housing costs is creating a nightmare scenario for families across the country.

Unless we act now—by demanding economic reforms, reproductive rights, and policies that address housing inequality—we are heading toward a dystopian future where millions of families are left homeless, and the American dream is dead.

This is not hyperbole. This is reality. And unless we confront it head-on, America will become a nation where the majority live in poverty, scraping by while a small elite wields all the power and wealth. We must fight for bodily autonomy, economic justice, and the rights of all people to live in a society that values them—not as servants, not as cogs in a machine, but as individuals with the right to self-determination and dignity.

Chapter 10: The Call to Action – Striking for Constitutional Change

The time has come for a radical, united movement to demand what is rightfully ours: the freedom and sovereignty over our own bodies, the autonomy to live our lives without being forced into marriages we do not want or pressured into childbirths we cannot afford. We must organize and execute a nationwide marriage and birth strike until the U.S. Constitution is amended to guarantee full bodily autonomy for every person, once and for all.

This movement must be large, loud, and unrelenting. It will require unprecedented solidarity across races, classes, and regions, because only together can we create the critical mass needed to force change. We outline the practical steps for organizing the strike, from facing down family pressure to persuading our partners to join us. This is not a time for politeness or half-measures. The stakes are too high, and we cannot afford to be nice about it anymore. This is a battle for the future of our bodies, our families, and our country.

Building Solidarity Across Races, Classes, and Regions

One of the greatest challenges facing any social movement is the ability to unite people from different backgrounds. Women from different races, social classes, and regions may face different struggles, but we are all affected by the erosion of our rights. This strike cannot succeed unless it draws on the collective power of women from all walks of life. Solidarity is essential.

Women of color, particularly Black, Indigenous, and Latina women, have historically faced the harshest consequences of inequality in the U.S. reproductive system. They are more likely to experience restricted access to healthcare, economic instability, and the fallout from forced birth policies. These women must be at the forefront of the movement, as their leadership will ensure that the strike addresses the needs of those most affected.

Similarly, working-class women, who often cannot afford the luxury of time or resources for political activism, must be supported by their wealthier sisters. Solidarity means recognizing that privilege varies and that those who have more must support those with less. This includes sharing financial resources, offering childcare, and providing emotional support during the strike.

Finally, women in urban centers and rural communities must come together, despite the political and cultural divides that often separate them. Women in rural areas may face unique challenges, such as more conservative social pressures and fewer resources, but they are critical to the movement's success. The strike must reach every corner of the country if it is to force real change.

Protecting Yourself Financially and Emotionally During the Strike

A marriage and birth strike is not a decision to be taken lightly. It requires preparation, both financial and emotional, to withstand the inevitable pushback from family, friends, and society at large. Here are some practical steps to help you protect yourself:

1 **Financial Preparation:**

- **Build a savings cushion.** Before embarking on the strike, aim to set aside as much savings as you can. This will give you the freedom to walk away from any financial dependency you might have, whether it's from a parent, partner, or job that's unsupportive of the movement.
- **Explore remote or freelance work.** Being financially independent during the strike is critical. Look for opportunities that allow for flexibility and minimize reliance on employers or industries that might punish your activism.
- **Create networks of mutual aid.** Women must support each other during the strike. Organize local networks where participants can share resources, whether that's housing, food, childcare, or money. Mutual aid will help everyone stay afloat during this period of disruption.

2 **Emotional Preparation:**

- **Set boundaries with family and friends.** Be prepared for backlash from loved ones who don't understand or agree with your participation in the strike. Make it clear that you will not entertain guilt trips, emotional manipulation, or pressure to back down.
- **Join support groups.** Look for or create support groups of like-minded women who are also participating in the strike. These groups

will provide you with emotional strength, solidarity, and a sense of community when the pressure becomes intense.

- **Therapy and counseling.** If possible, seek professional support to help you navigate the emotional challenges of going against societal expectations, especially if the pushback from family or loved ones becomes overwhelming.

Facing Down Your Parents: The Hard Conversation

Many women will face their greatest resistance not from society at large but from within their own families. Parents may pressure their daughters to marry and have children, often because of their own desires for grandchildren or societal expectations. This is where the hard conversations come in, and you must be prepared to stand firm.

Here are some key points to make to your parents:

1 **No Weddings, No Grandbabies.**

- **Be clear and unwavering.** Tell your parents that until there is a constitutional amendment guaranteeing your bodily autonomy, you will not marry or have children. Make it clear that their dreams of weddings and grandchildren are on hold, and that only by supporting this movement will they see that happen.

2 **They Need You More Than You Need Them.**

- **Social security and future support.** Many parents rely on the expectation that their children will support them in their old age. Remind them that without your financial security, independence, and autonomy, you may not be in a position to help them when they need it most. A country where women are forced into marriage and motherhood won't provide the economic foundation for daughters to care for aging parents.

- **Their self-interest.** Parents often act in their perceived self-interest, so make it clear that supporting your autonomy is in their best interest. By helping you fight for your rights, they are ensuring a stable, prosperous future where you will have the freedom to support them when the time comes.

3 **Appeal to Their Legacy.**

- **Creating a better future.** Frame your argument around the idea that they should want to leave a better world for their children and grandchildren. By supporting the fight for constitutional change, they are helping to create a society that values equality and autonomy, which will benefit future generations.

Swaying Your Partner: Bringing Your Spouse or Fiancé Onboard

Convincing your partner to support the strike may require a different approach. Many men feel personally attacked when confronted with the idea of a marriage and birth strike, as it can challenge their deeply ingrained expectations about family roles and the purpose of relationships. But with the right strategy, you can show them that the strike is not about punishing men but about creating a better, more equal future for everyone.

Here's how to frame the conversation:

1 **A Stronger, More Equal Family.**

- **Equality benefits everyone.** Explain that the strike is about ensuring that your family, and all families, are built on mutual respect and equality. Tell your partner that you want to create a relationship where both partners have autonomy and share responsibilities equally. This is not about rejecting marriage or children forever; it's about fighting for the right to make those decisions freely.
- **A better future for your children.** If you plan to have children together in the future, argue that it's in their best interest to be born into a world where women have full autonomy. Children will thrive in families where both parents are equals, and where women have the ability to pursue careers, education, and personal goals without societal pressure.

2 **The Economic Argument:**

- **No one can afford to raise a family in this economy.** Lay out the harsh economic realities. The cost of living has skyrocketed, and most families can no longer survive on two incomes, let alone one. Bringing children into this world without the financial security that equality provides is irresponsible. Your partner must understand that without the economic reforms that come from equal rights, raising a family will be an immense burden.

- **The benefits of delayed marriage and childbirth.** Studies show that couples who marry and have children later in life tend to be more financially secure and emotionally prepared. By delaying these decisions and focusing on the fight for equality, you're setting up your future family for long-term success.

3 **The Bigger Picture:**

- **Society as a whole benefits.** Point out that when women are free and equal, society becomes more prosperous. Men, too, benefit from living in a world where their partners are not subjugated but empowered. By supporting the strike, your partner will be helping to create a stronger, healthier society where families can thrive without the burdens of inequality.

The Demand for an Amendment: What Must Be Included

The ultimate goal of the marriage and birth strike is a constitutional amendment guaranteeing the inviolability of personal sovereignty over one's body. This amendment must go beyond mere lip service to women's rights—it must enshrine in law the full autonomy of every individual to make decisions about their body, free from government interference.

The amendment should include the following:

1 **Guaranteed Reproductive Rights:**

- The right to access contraception, abortion, and other reproductive healthcare must be protected. Women must have full control over their reproductive choices, free from government restrictions or coercion.

2 **Protection from Forced Medical Procedures:**

- No individual should be forced to undergo any medical procedure, including pregnancy or childbirth, without their explicit consent.

3 **The Right to Bodily Integrity:**

- Every person must have the right to make decisions about their own body, including gender-affirming care, medical treatments, and the right to refuse procedures or treatments.

4 **Equal Legal Protections:**

- The amendment must ensure that all individuals, regardless of gender, are granted equal legal protections, including the right to pursue careers, education, and personal fulfillment without discrimination or societal pressure.

5 **Criminalization of Coercion:**

- The amendment should criminalize any attempt to coerce individuals into marriage, pregnancy, or any other life-altering decision. This includes legal protections from familial or societal coercion, ensuring that every individual's autonomy is respected at all ages.

Strike Until We Win

The marriage and birth strike is not a temporary protest—it is a battle for the future of women's rights in America. Until we achieve a constitutional amendment guaranteeing full bodily autonomy, we must withhold our labor, our participation, and our bodies from a system that does not respect us. This movement will not succeed unless women, across races, classes, and regions, stand together in solidarity.

We must be prepared for the hard conversations with our families and partners, and we must stand firm in our demand for a better future. This is not about rejecting marriage or motherhood forever—it's about fighting for the right to make those choices freely, without coercion or oppression.

We are striking not just for ourselves but for the generations that will come after us. Together, we can demand the change that will create a society where every person is free to live their life on their own terms. And we will not stop until we win.

Chapter 11: Building the Future – A Society with Full Bodily Autonomy

Imagine a society where every person, regardless of gender, has full sovereignty over their body, where the decision to marry, have children, or pursue any personal or professional path is made without external pressure or coercion. This vision of the future may seem utopian, but it is entirely achievable—and many progressive societies around the world have already laid the groundwork. Enshrining bodily autonomy in the U.S. Constitution would not only empower women; it would revolutionize our culture, improve our legal system, and create a more just, prosperous, and fulfilled society for all.

Global Examples of Progress Through Bodily Autonomy

Countries that have embraced women's autonomy, gender equality, and reproductive rights are some of the most prosperous, peaceful, and happy nations in the world. These examples demonstrate how prioritizing equality and bodily autonomy leads to better societal outcomes, not just for women but for families, economies, and overall well-being.

Scandinavian Countries: The Pinnacle of Equality

Scandinavian nations, including **Norway**, **Sweden**, **Finland**, and **Denmark**, are frequently cited as models of equality. These countries consistently rank at the top of global happiness indexes and boast some of the best standards of living in the world. One of the key reasons for their success is the integration of gender equality and bodily autonomy into their social fabric.

113

In **Sweden**, for example, women's reproductive rights are fully protected, and access to abortion and contraception is guaranteed. The government provides comprehensive parental leave policies that allow both men and women to share in the responsibility of raising children. A 2019 study by the *World Economic Forum* ranked Sweden as one of the most gender-equal countries in the world, noting that this equality contributes significantly to the nation's high levels of happiness and economic stability.

Similarly, **Norway**'s commitment to equality has led to strong economic outcomes. According to the *World Happiness Report*, Norway consistently ranks among the happiest countries, with a strong social safety net, low levels of inequality, and a high degree of trust in institutions. Gender equality plays a key role in this success: Norwegian policies guarantee women's reproductive rights, ensure equal pay for equal work, and provide affordable childcare. Men benefit too, as these policies promote shared responsibility in the home and workplace, reducing the burden on any single individual.

The economic benefits of equality are clear. According to research by **McKinsey & Company**, advancing gender equality could add up to $12 trillion to global GDP by 2025. When women are free to participate fully in the workforce, economies grow and societies become more resilient. In countries like Finland, Norway, and Denmark, the integration of women into the workforce and political sphere has led to robust economic growth, innovative social policies, and high quality of life.

Iceland: Leading by Example in Gender Equality

Iceland has been at the forefront of gender equality for decades. In 1980, **Vigdís Finnbogadóttir** became the world's first democratically elected female president, a monumental achievement in a nation that had already begun to prioritize women's rights. Iceland's progressive policies have created a society where gender does not limit one's opportunities or autonomy.

In 1975, Icelandic women organized a nationwide strike to protest wage inequality and gender discrimination, which led to significant legal and social reforms. This act of collective resistance transformed the nation and led to long-term benefits for both women and men. Today, Iceland ranks first on the *Global Gender Gap Report* by the **World Economic Forum**, with women holding significant political power, equal access to education, and full reproductive rights.

One of the most notable effects of this progress is how it benefits men as well. With women fully integrated into society, men in Iceland enjoy more flexible work arrangements, greater involvement in their children's lives, and a higher quality of life overall. Men in progressive countries like Iceland are able to share both the responsibilities and the rewards of family life, which contributes to lower levels of stress, better mental health outcomes, and stronger family bonds.

New Zealand: Political Leadership and Bodily Autonomy

Under the leadership of **Jacinda Ardern**, New Zealand has become a shining example of how female leadership and a commitment to equality can shape a nation's future. Ardern has championed women's rights, including reproductive rights, and her government's response to crises such as the COVID-19 pandemic was hailed for its compassion, transparency, and effectiveness.

New Zealand legalized abortion in 2020, enshrining bodily autonomy as a fundamental right for women. This move was part of a broader push for equality in a country that has long prioritized women's rights—New Zealand was the first country to grant women the right to vote in 1893. Today, New Zealand ranks highly on the *Human Development Index,* with low levels of corruption, a high degree of social trust, and a robust economy.

The benefits of bodily autonomy are clear in New Zealand's success: women are free to make decisions about their reproductive health, men share in family responsibilities, and society as a whole benefits from a more equal distribution of power and opportunity.

Societal, Legal, and Cultural Shifts in a Fully Equal Society

The adoption of bodily autonomy in the U.S. would require profound societal, legal, and cultural shifts, but the benefits would be transformative. Such a society would be built on the principles of equality, respect, and personal freedom, where every individual—regardless of gender—has the right to control their own body and destiny.

Legal Changes: Protecting Autonomy and Equality

The legal landscape in a society with full bodily autonomy would guarantee reproductive rights, equal pay for equal work, and legal protections against discrimination. A constitutional amendment enshrining bodily autonomy would ensure that no government, religious institution, or other external force could interfere with an individual's right to make decisions about their own body. This would extend beyond reproductive rights to include the right to access healthcare, the right to refuse medical treatment, and the right to gender-affirming care.

By removing legal obstacles to equality, the law would support a society where individuals are empowered to pursue their personal, professional, and family goals without fear of discrimination or coercion. A society that values bodily autonomy would ensure equal access to education, healthcare, and economic opportunities for all, creating a more just and equitable system.

Cultural Shifts: Redefining Gender Roles and Family Structures

Culturally, a society with full bodily autonomy would see a redefinition of gender roles and family structures. The patriarchal expectation that women must serve as primary caregivers and homemakers would be replaced by a model of shared responsibility, where both men and women participate equally in parenting, household duties, and professional life.

Men would no longer be pressured to be the sole breadwinners or feel the weight of societal expectations to dominate the household. In progressive societies like Norway and Iceland, men are encouraged to take parental leave, share in domestic responsibilities, and support their partners in both personal and professional ambitions. This cultural shift has led to stronger, more resilient families where both partners are empowered and fulfilled.

Research shows that when men participate equally in childcare and household responsibilities, family dynamics improve, and children benefit from better emotional development. A 2018 study from the **American Psychological Association** found that children who grow up in households with equal parenting roles exhibit higher self-esteem, better academic performance, and stronger social skills.

Societal Benefits: A More Just and Prosperous Nation

The long-term benefits of a society that values bodily autonomy and gender equality are profound. Economically, the full participation of women in the workforce would drive innovation, boost productivity, and create a more competitive economy. According to a **World Bank** report, gender equality in the labor market could increase a nation's GDP by up to 30%.

Socially, equality would lead to healthier relationships, lower divorce rates, and reduced domestic violence. When both partners in a relationship have autonomy and equal rights, they are more likely to communicate openly, share responsibilities, and build stronger, more supportive relationships. In a society where women are not forced into unwanted pregnancies or marriages, the psychological and emotional well-being of families improves significantly.

As male historian **Steven Pinker** wrote in his book *The Better Angels of Our Nature*:

> "The empowerment of women, by giving them control over their lives and their bodies, is one of the most important forces for peace and prosperity in the modern world."

Historian **Yuval Noah Harari**, in *Sapiens*, also noted the immense benefits that come from gender equality:

> "The key to modern prosperity is not brute force but the ability to cooperate and share knowledge, and this is why societies that have embraced gender equality are flourishing."

A Future Worth Fighting For

Enshrining bodily autonomy in the U.S. Constitution would lead to a society where every person—man or woman—is free to make decisions about their own life, body, and future. This societal shift would bring about profound legal, cultural, and economic changes, leading to a more prosperous, just, and fulfilled nation. The benefits of such a revolution are already visible in progressive countries around the world, where equality has led to happier, healthier, and more resilient societies.

The time has come for America to embrace this future, to build a society where bodily autonomy is not a privilege but a fundamental right. By ensuring that all people have the

119

freedom to control their own bodies and make decisions about their lives, we will create a stronger, more equitable America—one that is better for women, better for families, and better for everyone.

Chapter 12: The Business Case for Gender Equality – Why Equality is the Key to Success

In the capitalist system, business is often the driving force behind social, political, and economic movements. Corporations, as powerful entities, influence not just markets but the lives of millions of employees. Historically, businesses have exploited the gender gap by paying women less and punishing them for taking time off for reproductive healthcare or family responsibilities. This approach has been touted as a cost-saving measure, a way to boost short-term profits. But this mindset is fundamentally flawed and, in reality, it is holding American businesses back.

We will dismantle the argument that gender inequality benefits businesses. With every available fact, figure, and example from around the world, we will prove that promoting gender equality in the workplace is not just the right thing to do—it's good business. Companies that have embraced gender equity, paid family leave, and fair pay for women have seen enormous financial gains. It's time for American businesses to recognize that inequality is a roadblock to success, and gender equality is the key to long-term profitability, innovation, and global competitiveness.

The Gender Pay Gap Hurts Business

One of the most pervasive myths in corporate America is that paying women less is a necessary evil to remain competitive. This is based on the outdated belief that women's labor is less valuable, particularly because of the possibility of maternity leave or childcare responsibilities.

However, this short-sighted approach is costing businesses far more than they realize.

According to a study from the **World Economic Forum**, the global gender pay gap currently stands at 20%, with women earning 80 cents for every dollar a man earns for similar work. In the United States, this gap is even wider for women of color. This disparity not only harms women—it harms businesses by creating environments where talent is undervalued and underutilized.

A **McKinsey & Company** report, *Women in the Workplace 2020*, found that companies with greater gender diversity, particularly in leadership, are more likely to outperform their competitors. Firms in the top quartile for gender diversity in executive teams are 25% more likely to have above-average profitability than companies in the bottom quartile. This is no coincidence—when women are compensated fairly and promoted based on their abilities, they bring unique perspectives that drive innovation and business success.

The cost of maintaining the gender pay gap is not limited to employee dissatisfaction—it also leads to higher turnover rates. According to a study from **Boston Consulting Group**, companies with poor gender diversity see much higher employee churn. Replacing employees is expensive, costing businesses 6 to 9 months of a worker's salary on average, including recruitment, training, and lost productivity. By closing the gender pay gap and providing equal opportunities for advancement, businesses can reduce turnover and retain top talent.

Women's Equality Drives Innovation

One of the strongest arguments for gender equality in the workplace is its impact on innovation. Numerous studies have shown that diverse teams produce more creative solutions and are better equipped to solve complex problems. This is especially true in industries that rely on innovation, such as technology, finance, and healthcare.

A **Harvard Business Review** article on diversity and innovation revealed that companies with diverse workforces are 45% more likely to report market share growth over the previous year and are 70% more likely to capture new markets. This is because diverse teams bring a variety of perspectives, ideas, and problem-solving approaches, which leads to more innovative products and services.

One standout example of the business case for gender diversity is **SAP**, the German software giant. SAP implemented a gender diversity program aimed at increasing the number of women in leadership roles. As a result, SAP saw an increase in innovation and a 50% improvement in employee engagement scores. Their internal study showed that teams with more women in leadership had higher sales performance and customer satisfaction ratings. SAP's experience demonstrates that when women are included at the highest levels of decision-making, the entire company benefits from increased creativity and better business outcomes.

Similarly, **Johnson & Johnson**, a global healthcare company, has been a leader in gender equality in the workplace. Johnson & Johnson's commitment to promoting women at all levels of the organization has led to numerous innovations in medical devices and pharmaceuticals. In 2018, Johnson & Johnson was named to the *DiversityInc* Top 50 Companies for Diversity list, and their focus on diversity and inclusion has been credited with driving the company's growth in global markets.

Paid Family Leave and Work-Life Balance: A Win-Win for Business

The fear that maternity leave or family responsibilities will diminish a woman's contribution to the workplace is not only unfounded—it is harmful to businesses. Countries that have adopted comprehensive paid family leave policies and created work-life balance programs have seen their businesses flourish. These policies benefit not only women but all employees by creating a healthier, more productive workforce.

Sweden provides one of the best examples of the benefits of paid family leave. In Sweden, parents are entitled to 480 days of paid parental leave, which can be shared between both parents. This policy not only helps women return to work after having children, but it also encourages men to take a more active role in caregiving. Companies in Sweden have found that paid family leave increases employee loyalty, reduces absenteeism, and improves overall job satisfaction.

A **Swedish Institute** report found that businesses in Sweden experience higher productivity and lower turnover as a result of their generous parental leave policies. Employees who take time off for family responsibilities are more likely to return to work refreshed and motivated, reducing burnout and increasing long-term productivity. The return on investment for these programs is substantial—businesses benefit from lower training and recruitment costs, higher employee engagement, and a healthier work environment.

In the United States, some companies are beginning to recognize the benefits of offering paid family leave. **Etsy**, the online marketplace for handmade goods, implemented a generous paid parental leave policy that allows all employees —regardless of gender—to take 26 weeks of paid leave. The result? Etsy has one of the lowest employee turnover rates in the tech industry and consistently ranks as one of the best places to work. Their paid family leave policy has created a more loyal, engaged workforce and has helped attract top talent.

Another example comes from **Google**, which extended its paid maternity leave from 12 weeks to 18 weeks in 2007. This change led to a 50% reduction in the rate at which new mothers left the company. By recognizing that work-life balance is essential to employee retention and satisfaction, Google has reaped the benefits of a more stable and productive workforce.

Gender Equality Is Good for Shareholders and Investors

For publicly traded companies, gender equality is not just a social issue—it's a financial imperative. A growing body of research shows that companies with diverse leadership teams deliver higher returns to shareholders.

Investors are increasingly recognizing that diversity is a key indicator of long-term financial success.

A 2020 study by **MSCI**, a leading provider of investment decision support tools, found that companies with strong gender diversity on their boards outperformed those without it by 36% in terms of return on equity. Similarly, a **Credit Suisse** report revealed that companies with more women in decision-making positions had higher profitability and stock performance than their less-diverse peers.

Institutional investors are taking notice. **BlackRock**, the world's largest asset manager, has begun pressuring companies in its portfolio to improve gender diversity at the board level. In its 2021 annual letter to CEOs, BlackRock emphasized the importance of diversity and inclusion, warning that companies failing to prioritize these issues could face shareholder backlash. The message is clear: gender equality is not just a moral imperative—it's a financial one.

Global Competitiveness: America Is Falling Behind

While some American companies are making progress on gender equality, the U.S. as a whole is falling behind. In countries like **Norway**, where gender diversity is mandated by law, businesses are seeing significant gains in competitiveness and profitability. The **World Economic Forum**'s *Global Gender Gap Report* ranks Norway as one of the most gender-equal countries in the world, and its businesses are thriving as a result.

By contrast, the U.S. ranks 53rd in gender equality, according to the same report. This lag is not just a social issue

—it's an economic one. A lack of gender equality is costing American businesses billions of dollars in lost productivity, turnover, and missed opportunities. If the U.S. wants to remain competitive in the global marketplace, it must prioritize gender equality and create policies that support women's full participation in the workforce.

The **International Monetary Fund** (IMF) has also weighed in on the economic benefits of gender equality. According to the IMF, if the U.S. were to close its gender gap, it could increase its GDP by 5%. The IMF's research shows that when women are able to participate fully in the labor market, they bring new skills, ideas, and innovation to the economy, driving growth and competitiveness.

The Future of Business: Embracing Gender Equality for Long-Term Success

The evidence is overwhelming: businesses that embrace gender equality are more successful, more innovative, and more profitable. The outdated belief that women are a burden to businesses—whether because of family responsibilities or the myth of lower productivity—is not only wrong, but it is also costing companies billions of dollars in lost opportunities.

It's time for American businesses to recognize that gender equality is not a nice-to-have—it's a must-have. Companies that fail to prioritize equality are not just doing a disservice to their female employees; they are holding themselves back from reaching their full potential. By closing the gender pay gap, offering paid family leave, and promoting women into leadership roles, businesses can create a more innovative, productive, and successful future.

Gender Equality Is the Key to Business Success

American businesses stand at a crossroads. They can continue down the path of inequality, risking turnover, lost productivity, and underperformance, or they can embrace gender equality and reap the rewards of a more dynamic, innovative, and successful workforce. The choice is clear: inequality is bad for business, and gender equality is the key to long-term success.

From the thriving businesses of Scandinavia to the innovative companies in New Zealand and the shareholder-driven markets of the U.S., the message is consistent: when women succeed, businesses succeed. It's time for American businesses to recognize that investing in gender equality is not just about doing the right thing—it's about building a better, more profitable future for everyone.

Chapter 13: The Fertility Crisis, Microplastics, and the False Promises of Forced Birth

The world is facing an unprecedented fertility crisis. Between declining birth rates, dropping sperm counts, and the disturbing presence of microplastics in human reproductive tissues, the ability to conceive is under threat in ways never seen before. A recent viral article titled "Sperm Counts Drop by 62% Worldwide" highlights a shocking reality: sperm counts have plummeted by 62% between 1973 and 2018, signaling a potential reproductive catastrophe. The referenced study, published in the journal *Human Reproduction Update*, raises alarms that this drop is not just a regional anomaly but a global trend that could lead to widespread infertility.

Against this backdrop, the push for forced birth policies—mandating that women carry pregnancies to term regardless of their health or personal circumstances—appears not only cruel but deeply irrational. We are on the verge of a fertility crisis, and the solution is not to further restrict access to reproductive healthcare. On the contrary, now more than ever, technologies such as in vitro fertilization (IVF) and comprehensive reproductive health services must be protected, expanded, and made universally accessible. We must safeguard the right of all people to make decisions about their reproductive health, as this is the only way we can hope to mitigate the catastrophic decline in fertility rates.

As we face the uncertain future brought about by microplastics, environmental toxins, and a healthcare system increasingly catering to profit rather than care, one thing is certain: forced birth policies will only exacerbate the situation. A national-level abortion ban would likely lead to a surge in women seeking permanent sterilization, a choice from which we may never recover in terms of future birth rates. The very idea of treating women as mere vessels for reproduction, as though we are nothing more than "breeding stock," is not only deeply offensive but fundamentally harmful to the survival of our society. Women are not tools to bolster nationalist agendas, and we must reject this dehumanizing ideology before it does irreversible damage.

The Fertility Crisis: Microplastics and Declining Reproductive Health

The global fertility crisis is not an abstract problem. It is happening now, and the numbers are alarming. In the last five decades, sperm counts among men have dropped by 62%, according to a comprehensive study published in *Human Reproduction Update*. The causes of this decline are multifaceted, with environmental toxins like microplastics being major contributors. Microplastics—tiny plastic particles found in everything from food packaging to personal care products—are now infiltrating human bodies at a cellular level. Studies have detected microplastics in both male and female reproductive tissues, raising serious concerns about the long-term impact on fertility.

Microplastics disrupt hormonal balances and interfere with reproductive development. For men, they can lead to decreased sperm production and motility, while for women, microplastics are linked to higher risks of miscarriage, reduced ovarian function, and complications during pregnancy. According to a 2022 report by the *National*

Institutes of Health (NIH), environmental pollutants, including microplastics, are major factors contributing to the rising rates of infertility and pregnancy complications.

The damage being done by microplastics and other environmental toxins may take generations to clean up, and in the meantime, we must take all possible measures to protect our reproductive futures. Comprehensive reproductive healthcare, including access to fertility treatments like IVF, is essential. Yet, instead of addressing the real threats to reproductive health, lawmakers in several states are focusing on restricting access to abortion and reproductive care. This misguided focus will do nothing to reverse declining fertility rates; it will only drive women away from the healthcare system entirely.

Rising Rates of Sterilization and the Impact on Future Birth Rates

As reproductive rights are stripped away, an increasing number of women are choosing permanent sterilization. In the United States, the number of women opting for sterilization has surged in recent years. This is not a coincidence—it is a direct response to the fear that women will lose control over their own bodies in a system where forced birth becomes the law of the land.

According to data from the **Guttmacher Institute**, the number of women seeking sterilization has risen sharply since the overturning of *Roe v. Wade*. In 2021 alone, the rate of sterilization increased by 24% among women in their twenties and thirties. For many women, sterilization represents the only way to guarantee they won't be forced into a pregnancy that could endanger their health or financial security. These are women who might otherwise have had children in the future but are now permanently opting out of motherhood because of the dangerous climate surrounding reproductive rights.

The more we restrict reproductive healthcare, the more we push women to permanently remove themselves from the breeding population. This has serious implications for the future birth rate of the U.S., which is already at historic lows. The U.S. fertility rate was just 1.64 births per woman in 2020, well below the replacement level of 2.1 needed to maintain population stability, according to the **Centers for Disease Control and Prevention (CDC)**. The fewer women willing to participate in a system that may kill them or deny them their rights, the further our birth rate will fall.

This trend is not just affecting individual women—it is creating a demographic crisis. With fewer women choosing to have children, the American labor force will shrink, the tax base will contract, and the economic burden of an aging population will increase. Ironically, the forced birth movement, driven by nationalist desires to increase the white birth rate, is likely to have the opposite effect. Women who feel their rights are under attack are choosing permanent sterilization, and future generations will pay the price.

Forced Birth: A False Solution to the Declining Birth Rate

The forced birth movement is rooted in the false belief that restricting abortion will somehow reverse the declining birth rate. This is not only factually incorrect but also deeply misguided. Abortion bans do not create more babies—they create more suffering, for both women and the children they are forced to have. As abortion becomes more difficult to access, women are increasingly opting out of reproduction entirely.

We are also seeing a surge in women choosing to adopt rather than have biological children in a country where forced birth policies threaten their lives. Ironically, many of these adoptions are likely to come from poor countries with majority non-white populations. This runs directly counter to the nationalist agenda of increasing the white birth rate, as articulated by figures like Representative **Mary Miller**, who famously called the overturning of *Roe v. Wade* a "historic victory for white life." Her statement revealed the dark motivations behind the forced birth movement: a desire to force middle-class white women to bear more children in order to preserve a certain demographic majority.

This vision of treating women as nothing more than breeding stock is beyond reprehensible. It reduces women to mere tools for perpetuating a racial or national agenda, stripping them of their humanity and autonomy. Such an ideology is not only ethically abhorrent but also counterproductive. The more we force women into unwanted pregnancies, the more likely they are to opt out of motherhood altogether, through sterilization or other means.

The Decline of Healthcare and the Danger to Women

The decline in fertility is exacerbated by a broader collapse in the quality of healthcare in America. Our healthcare system is increasingly driven by profit, with breakthroughs in medicine reserved for the wealthy while the general population suffers. The life expectancy of the American worker is declining year by year, and the health outcomes for women, in particular, are worsening.

A report by the **Commonwealth Fund** found that the U.S. has the highest maternal mortality rate among developed countries, and the situation is only getting worse. In 2020, the maternal mortality rate rose to 23.8 deaths per 100,000 live births, with Black women dying at three times the rate of white women. This is not a country where women feel safe bringing children into the world, and it's no wonder so many are opting out of motherhood.

The idea of forcing women to give birth in a country with declining healthcare standards and a skyrocketing maternal mortality rate is not just irresponsible—it is criminal. No one can be faulted for putting their own life over the risk of dying in childbirth, especially in a system that prioritizes profit over care.

Rejecting the Dehumanizing Ideology of Forced Birth

At the heart of the forced birth movement is a dehumanizing ideology that treats women as mere vessels for reproduction. This is an ideology that must be rejected in the strongest terms. Women are not breeding animals, and they are not tools for increasing the population of any particular demographic. We are human beings, deserving of respect, autonomy, and the right to make decisions about our own bodies.

The forced birth movement is doing irreparable harm to the birth rate in the United States, and it will only get worse if we continue down this path. A national abortion ban would drive millions of women to choose permanent sterilization or adoption from foreign countries, leading to a demographic collapse and a further weakening of our society. This is not a sustainable future—it is a dystopian one.

A Declaration of Autonomy and Humanity

Women deserve to be treated as humans, as equals, and as individuals with the right to make decisions about their own bodies. We are not breeding stock for nationalist agendas. We are not tools to be used and discarded by a system that cares more about maintaining power than it does about our lives.

We demand the right to full bodily autonomy, the right to access reproductive healthcare, and the right to decide when, how, and if we want to bring children into this world. We are not asking for favors—we are demanding the respect that every human being deserves. It is time to reject the forced birth movement and to embrace a future where women are free, safe, and empowered to make decisions that protect their health, their dignity, and their future.

Chapter 14: Out of time and it's now or never?

Alternative: Pregnancy Tourism as a Safer Choice for Mothers

Opening with the idea of "pregnancy tourism" as a strategy for mothers seeking safer, more affordable maternal care than what's currently available in the U.S. This term can introduce readers to the concept of temporarily relocating to countries with superior maternal healthcare to ensure a safe and supported birth experience.

Imagine a place where maternal healthcare is not just more affordable but safer. Pregnancy tourism isn't a luxury; it's a lifeline for mothers who want the best for themselves and their babies.

Imagine transforming the experience of pregnancy and birth into something extraordinary—a journey to a country where quality healthcare, serenity, and support surround you every step of the way. This is the promise of pregnancy tourism. Far from the typical stress and costs associated with childbirth in the U.S., pregnancy tourism offers expecting mothers a unique opportunity: to nurture their health and bond with their baby in a place that prioritizes care, comfort, and peace of mind.

Instead of rushing to prenatal appointments squeezed between work obligations, picture yourself strolling through a peaceful, scenic city in a country known for its world-class healthcare. You might be in the French countryside, with its rolling lavender fields and charming villages, or near a Scandinavian lake surrounded by fresh air and mountains. Imagine the difference in experiencing a relaxed, leisurely pregnancy where each day is focused on your well-being. Many of these countries offer generous maternity programs that prioritize maternal health, preventive care, and stress-free pregnancies, which contribute to a safer and happier experience for both mother and child.

Pregnancy tourism allows you to take a step back from the hectic pace of life and focus on what truly matters. It's a break from the endless paperwork and stress of insurance and hospital bills. It's a chance to be pampered, with access to well-trained midwives, birthing centers with home-like atmospheres, and prenatal specialists ready to guide you through each stage of pregnancy. In these countries, expecting mothers are given abundant care options, from comprehensive prenatal checkups to soothing therapies like prenatal massage, yoga, and lactation guidance. Imagine a birth experience where every detail is designed with the mother's comfort in mind—clean, private facilities, personalized care, and the freedom to choose the birth plan that aligns with your values.

By spending these transformative months abroad, pregnancy becomes a journey you'll always remember fondly—a true "pregnancy vacation." You're not just a patient; you're an honored guest in a country that respects motherhood, views birth as sacred, and has crafted systems to support every woman's unique needs. This experience could include touring the sights in your new city, sampling local foods, and perhaps

137

learning a bit of a new language, enriching both you and your child's future with memories of a place that was their first home.

For many American mothers, pregnancy can feel rushed and medicalized, with doctors often focused on efficiency over empathy. But in countries that rank high in maternal healthcare, your care team will likely include skilled midwives, lactation consultants, and practitioners who take the time to get to know you and your needs. This comprehensive care not only makes your pregnancy smoother but can foster an environment where you feel nurtured and valued as a new mother. Countries like Sweden, the Netherlands, and Canada offer support at every stage, from pregnancy through postpartum, with a focus on holistic well-being. Imagine a pregnancy and birth experience where each moment feels intentional, every need is met, and your memories are of calm, joyful moments, not anxieties about costs or care gaps.

These months abroad could mark the start of a lifetime's worth of memories, shared by both parents and child. Imagine looking back on your pregnancy as a time of adventure and relaxation, far from the grind of work and constant medical fees. When your child is old enough, you'll have stories to tell about where they were born, the city or village that first welcomed them into the world. Perhaps you'll even return to that place someday, showing your child the beautiful surroundings where their journey began—a place chosen not just for safety, but for the beauty, peace, and supportive care it offered you during those life-changing months.

Choosing pregnancy tourism is a decision to prioritize your own well-being and happiness during one of life's most meaningful moments. It's an opportunity to embrace pregnancy as an experience worth cherishing, free from the stress and financial burdens of the American healthcare system. You deserve to feel celebrated and supported as you welcome a new life into the world, and with pregnancy tourism, your experience can be just as enriching as it is safe. This isn't just a break from the norm; it's a choice to create lifelong memories that you and your family will treasure forever.

Maternal and Infant Mortality Rates in the U.S. vs. Other Countries

This is how maternal and infant mortality rates compare in the U.S. to countries with better statistics.

- **U.S. Maternal Mortality Rate:** According to the CDC, the U.S. has one of the highest maternal mortality rates among developed countries, at around 23.8 deaths per 100,000 live births. The rate has continued to rise, with Black women experiencing a threefold higher risk than white women.
- **Infant Mortality Rate:** In the U.S., the infant mortality rate is 5.6 deaths per 1,000 live births, higher than in other developed nations.

Countries with Significantly Lower Mortality Rates:

- **Finland** and **Norway**: Less than 3 maternal deaths per 100,000 live births.

- **Sweden** and **Denmark**: Between 3-4 maternal deaths per 100,000 live births.
- **Japan**: Approximately 5 maternal deaths per 100,000 live births.

These countries offer free or highly subsidized healthcare, reducing both maternal and infant mortality rates through accessible and thorough prenatal and postnatal care.

Quality of Maternal and Infant Medical Care in Top-Ranked Countries

Medical Care Quality:

- Countries like **Finland, Norway, and Sweden** consistently rank among the top for maternal care due to their preventive approach. Expecting mothers have access to regular checkups, home visits, lactation support, and emergency care when necessary.
- **Germany and the Netherlands**: Offer extensive maternal health programs, including prenatal screening and postnatal support through midwives and regular pediatric checkups for infants.

Costs of Giving Birth in Top Countries with Free Healthcare:

- **United Kingdom**: Most healthcare, including prenatal and birth-related expenses, is covered by the National Health Service (NHS).
- **France**: Provides free or low-cost healthcare with exceptional maternal care, allowing mothers to stay up to 4–5 days in the hospital post-birth.

In the U.S., average out-of-pocket costs for a normal delivery can exceed $4,500, with C-sections and complications costing significantly more. Pregnancy tourism in these countries not only ensures high-quality care but reduces the financial burden on the family.

Paid Time Off Policies and Maternity Benefits in Countries with Superior Healthcare

Countries with free healthcare often also offer paid maternity leave, which ensures financial stability during the early months of a child's life:

- **Sweden**: Offers 480 days of parental leave, with 390 days paid at 80% of the parent's salary.
- **Germany**: Provides up to 14 months of paid parental leave at approximately 67% of previous earnings.
- **Norway**: Up to 49 weeks at full pay or 59 weeks at 80% pay.
- **Canada**: Offers 12-18 months of paid parental leave with varying levels of financial support.

These policies starkly contrast with the U.S., where only about 20% of private-sector workers have access to paid family leave. This level of support allows families to focus on their child's early development without the stress of immediate financial needs.

Work Visas and the Ease of Obtaining Employment in Maternal-Friendly Countries

Ease of Obtaining Work Visas in Maternal-Friendly Countries:

- **Canada**: Has a straightforward work visa program, especially for skilled workers. The Express Entry program allows eligible workers to obtain permanent residency in six months or less.
- **Germany**: Offers the EU Blue Card, designed to attract skilled workers from outside the EU, making it easier for qualified individuals to work and reside.
- **Australia**: Provides several work visa options and a healthcare system with strong maternal care support.
- **New Zealand**: Has visa programs for skilled workers and offers affordable maternal healthcare with additional support services.

Benefits of Pregnancy Tourism for Families and Host Countries

- **For Mothers and Babies**: Pregnancy tourism offers a chance for mothers to experience affordable, quality medical care that prioritizes safety and health without the overwhelming costs associated with U.S. healthcare. Families can save thousands of dollars while ensuring that they receive the best possible care.

- **For Host Countries**: The host country benefits from having skilled workers and their families contribute to the economy. They are gaining workers who participate in the economy, pay taxes, and contribute to the diversity and skills within the workforce.

Exploring Pregnancy Tourism as a Safer, Smarter Choice for New Families

Imagine a place where maternal healthcare is not only more affordable but safer and more supportive. For many mothers, pregnancy tourism isn't a luxury; it's a lifeline. Amid high maternal and infant mortality rates in the U.S., the choice to give birth abroad is becoming an attractive and even necessary option for families who want a healthier, safer start for their child.

Maternal and Infant Mortality Rates in the U.S. vs. Safer Countries

To understand why pregnancy tourism has become appealing, we first need to recognize the challenges facing maternal and infant health in the U.S. Despite advances in medical technology, America's maternal and infant mortality rates are alarmingly high—and rising.

Current Statistics in the U.S.:

- **Maternal Mortality Rate**: According to the CDC, the U.S. has one of the highest maternal mortality rates among developed countries, at approximately 23.8 deaths per 100,000 live births. Black women are at even greater risk, with a rate nearly three times that of white women.
- **Infant Mortality Rate**: The U.S. infant mortality rate is around 5.6 deaths per 1,000 live births, a troubling figure when compared to other developed nations.

Countries with Lower Mortality Rates and Better Healthcare:

143

- **Finland and Norway** report less than 3 maternal deaths per 100,000 live births, ranking among the safest places in the world to give birth.
- **Sweden and Denmark** are close, with mortality rates between 3–4 per 100,000 live births.
- **Japan** has a maternal mortality rate of around 5 per 100,000 live births.

These countries also report lower infant mortality rates, supported by proactive prenatal and postnatal care, free or affordable healthcare access, and an emphasis on preventive care for mothers and infants. By choosing these locations for childbirth, families can access safer, higher-quality care than they might receive in the U.S.

Quality of Maternal and Infant Medical Care in Top-Ranked Countries

In countries with superior maternal care, the healthcare system emphasizes safety, support, and thorough prenatal and postnatal care.

- **Finland, Norway, and Sweden**: These nations are leaders in maternal health. Expecting mothers have access to frequent checkups, home visits, lactation support, and emergency care as needed. Finnish hospitals, for instance, routinely provide prenatal classes, extended hospital stays after delivery, and follow-up checkups for both mother and baby.
- **Germany and the Netherlands**: Known for robust maternal programs, these countries offer comprehensive prenatal screening, midwifery support,

and routine pediatric care. Germany, in particular, supports new parents with home visits from healthcare providers to ensure a smooth transition to parenthood.

Cost Comparison:

- **United Kingdom**: Through the National Health Service (NHS), most maternal healthcare services are free or covered with minimal costs.
- **France**: Provides free or highly subsidized maternal care, including a four-to-five-day postnatal hospital stay, allowing mothers time to recover with professional support.

In contrast, families in the U.S. often face significant out-of-pocket costs. A typical hospital delivery averages around $4,500, and costs for C-sections or other complications can soar far higher. Pregnancy tourism to countries with affordable healthcare can save thousands while providing access to a safer and more supportive environment.

Work Visas and Employment Opportunities in Maternal-Friendly Countries

Many of the countries with the best maternal and infant healthcare are also welcoming to foreign workers, offering work visas that grant access to the same healthcare benefits as citizens.

- **Canada**: Through the Express Entry program, skilled workers can qualify for permanent residency in about six months, gaining access to the Canadian healthcare system, which includes maternal benefits.

- **Germany**: Offers the EU Blue Card to skilled non-EU citizens, allowing for work and residency. With this visa, foreign workers can access Germany's healthcare and social services.
- **Australia**: Provides work visas for skilled professionals, granting access to universal healthcare with affordable maternal services.
- **New Zealand**: Welcomes skilled foreign workers and offers a healthcare system with strong maternal support, ensuring affordable prenatal and delivery care.

Securing a work visa allows expecting parents to establish themselves financially while qualifying for high-quality maternal care and parental leave in these supportive healthcare systems.

Benefits of Pregnancy Tourism for Families and Host Countries

The advantages of pregnancy tourism extend beyond the immediate family, offering mutual benefits to the mother and the host country.

- **For Mothers and Families**: Pregnancy tourism allows families to experience affordable, high-quality medical care that prioritizes safety and reduces costs. Mothers and babies receive the support they need during a crucial period, saving families thousands of dollars and enabling a safer, healthier start.
- **For Host Countries**: Countries with welcoming work visa programs benefit from skilled workers who

actively contribute to the economy, pay taxes, and add
to the diversity and expertise of the workforce.
Pregnancy tourism is an investment in both the
family's future and the host country's economic and
social fabric.

A Pregnancy Vacation for the Whole Family: An Affordable, Life-Enriching Adventure Abroad

Imagine transforming your pregnancy into a journey that
benefits not just you but your whole family, a chance to
immerse yourselves in a new culture, embrace a slower pace
of life, and savor these precious months together. In countries
with generous maternal healthcare and family support
programs, a "pregnancy vacation" could be a cost-effective,
unforgettable experience, not just for you and your partner,
but for your children as well.

Many top-ranked healthcare countries offer comprehensive
family support, including subsidized or even free child care.
In places like Sweden, Denmark, and Canada, families with
young children can take advantage of highly affordable
daycare and early childhood programs. These nations see
child care as a right rather than a privilege, ensuring that
working parents can balance family and career without the
exorbitant costs often associated with child care in the U.S.
For a family spending months abroad, this means you could
work or enjoy your time with peace of mind, knowing your
child is in safe, enriching care that's not only affordable but
often fully covered as part of the benefits provided to
working residents.

Imagine settling in a charming European town or bustling Canadian city, where the cost of living is often lower than in major American cities like New York, San Francisco, or Los Angeles. Even with airfare expenses, your time abroad could easily match or even cost less than the price of a few months back home. In these countries, housing, food, and transportation costs are frequently lower, allowing your family to live comfortably on a moderate income while enjoying a high quality of life.

By spending these months together as a family in a supportive, family-friendly country, you're not only ensuring a safe pregnancy and a memorable birth experience but creating lasting memories. Weekends could be spent exploring beautiful parks, visiting historic sites, or participating in local festivals—activities that are often free or affordable and add so much richness to family life. For children, this is an invaluable opportunity to experience a new culture and broaden their horizons. Imagine how they'll tell stories about their "second home," the friends they made, the words they learned in a new language, or the flavors they tasted for the first time. You'll have a shared adventure that binds you closer, enriching your family bond through experiences beyond the routine.

The best part? Your experience abroad will be supported by a healthcare system that views families as a national priority, with policies designed to relieve stress and financial pressure on parents. In these countries, even your own healthcare costs during pregnancy are largely, if not entirely, covered. From prenatal care to postpartum support, you'll have access to services without the towering bills that often accompany childbirth in the U.S. You're making a choice that not only gives your family a unique experience but also provides the support you need to stay healthy, secure, and relaxed.

A pregnancy vacation is more than a trip; it's a chance to show your children a different way of life, a more connected, fulfilling experience that supports everyone's well-being. By taking this journey, you're creating lifelong memories and building a stronger foundation for your growing family. From health and safety to financial savings and cultural enrichment, the benefits of pregnancy tourism extend far beyond the birth itself. For many families, it's a once-in-a-lifetime experience —a perfect blend of adventure, affordability, and lasting joy that they'll carry with them forever.

Paid Time Off Policies and Maternity Benefits in Countries with Superior Healthcare

Beyond healthcare, many countries offer generous paid parental leave policies that ensure financial stability during the child's early months. These benefits can significantly reduce the stress and financial burden on new parents.

- **Sweden**: Parents are entitled to 480 days of leave per child, with 390 of those days paid at approximately 80% of the parent's income.
- **Germany**: Provides up to 14 months of paid parental leave, with each parent eligible for at least two months, paid at about 67% of their salary.

- **Norway**: Offers 49 weeks of parental leave at full pay or 59 weeks at 80% pay.
- **Canada**: Offers parental leave that ranges from 12 to 18 months, with financial support based on employment insurance.

These policies allow parents to focus on bonding with and caring for their newborn without financial stress. The U.S., by contrast, offers no federally mandated paid parental leave, leaving only 20% of private-sector workers with access to paid family leave. This discrepancy highlights the potential benefits of seeking employment and starting a family in a country where parental care is prioritized.

Family Planning and Long-Term Considerations

With potential restrictions on family planning in the U.S., it's crucial to consider options for long-term birth control if living or working abroad. Certain forms of contraception, such as oral contraceptives, may become harder to access if regulations increase. Long-term options like IUDs or implants offer reliable, extended protection and can provide a solution if other forms of birth control are restricted.

Considering a secure family planning method before leaving the U.S. is an essential step. By establishing family plans abroad, couples can protect their reproductive autonomy and make proactive choices for their future.

Making the safest Choice to Invest in Your Family's Health and Future

Pregnancy tourism is more than just a temporary relocation; it's a decision to prioritize your family's health, safety, and financial stability. In countries with lower maternal and infant mortality rates, generous parental leave, affordable healthcare, and strong visa programs, families find a nurturing environment to welcome their child into the world. By choosing pregnancy tourism, families invest in a safer, healthier start and a more secure future, making a world of difference for parents and children alike.

Choosing to have your baby in a country with proven maternal care and support is more than a practical decision—it's an empowering choice for you and your family. When you give birth in a country with top-tier healthcare, you ensure a safer, more comfortable environment during one of life's most critical moments. You protect your child's health, invest in your well-being, and give your family a foundation of stability and support that might otherwise feel out of reach.

Imagine a healthcare system where you don't have to worry about hidden costs or emergency fees. In countries with universal healthcare, the high-quality medical support you need is built into the system. Giving birth in these countries means immediate access to everything from prenatal checkups to postnatal care, ensuring a seamless and supportive experience. Without the strain of overwhelming medical bills, you can focus entirely on welcoming your new child into the world, free from the financial pressures that too often accompany childbirth in the U.S.

And it's not only about the moment of birth. Many countries also offer paid parental leave, so you and your partner can bond with your baby without worrying about lost income. Imagine spending those first few precious months with the financial backing to stay home, heal, and build strong family connections without the stress of rushing back to work. It's a priceless opportunity that impacts your child's earliest and most formative days.

Beyond the health benefits, these countries welcome skilled foreign workers, meaning you could contribute to the local economy and immerse yourself in a supportive, family-friendly environment. As a working resident, you receive the same medical care as any citizen. These nations prioritize families and health, allowing you to build a future without compromise.

By choosing pregnancy tourism, you're taking a proactive step for your family's well-being. You're not only ensuring a safer birth and a smoother recovery, but you're also investing in a healthier, more secure start for your child. For many, it's a life-changing decision—a chance to experience the support and care every parent deserves.

Chapter 15: A New Dawn for America – Rebuilding Our Nation with Equality

As we reach the end of this journey, the truth is unmistakable: this fight is not just about women. It is about the future of America. The struggle for bodily autonomy and gender equality is a battle for the soul of our nation. The freedoms we claim to hold dear—liberty, justice, and the pursuit of happiness—have been compromised for far too long, particularly for women. Our country's potential has been stifled by systemic inequality, and the time has come to lift ourselves out of this repression. It is time for America to live up to its founding ideals and build a future where equality is fully realized.

Women deserve nothing less than a safe, fair, and free world in which to bring the next generation into—a world that honors the monumental sacrifices they make in building the future. It is women who give their time, their energy, and their very bodies to nurture and sustain life. This act, this greatest of all works, is the cornerstone of any thriving society and should be respected and revered above all else. When we deprive women of the resources, rights, and autonomy they need to bring the next generation into the world safely and freely, we cannot expect them to continue participating in a system that treats them as less than equal.

No society can thrive while half of its population is shackled by unfair burdens, denied the right to make decisions about their own bodies, and forced into roles without respect for their labor. If our hands are tied—whether through restrictive laws or societal pressure—then our legs should remain electively closed. It is only logical. Why should women continue to take on the enormous responsibility of motherhood when they are denied the basic tools and freedoms needed to ensure the safety and health of themselves and their children?

This is not just a fight for women—it is a fight for all people who value fairness, respect, and partnership. Men who truly love and respect women, men who understand the importance of equal partnership in building a family, will naturally stand with us. They know that a strong family is built on a foundation of equality, where both partners have control over their own bodies and a say in their reproductive health.

For good men, the current system is as unfair as it is for women. They deserve a world where their partners are empowered, healthy, and supported in their choices. A world where decisions about family and reproduction are made in collaboration, not coercion. Yet, the same system that deprives women of their rights also deprives men of the tools they need to build strong, healthy families. When selfish actors—whether in politics, business, or society—manipulate the rules to favor those who hold no respect for women, it diminishes everyone's ability to create a healthy household.

The men who genuinely seek partnership and equality are also hurt by these unjust systems. They, too, want the freedom to make choices about their lives and their futures without interference from those who benefit from maintaining inequality. When women are denied their rights, men are denied the ability to build families on a foundation of respect, collaboration, and mutual care. This struggle is not just about women gaining autonomy—it is about creating a society where everyone, including men, can thrive in relationships built on trust, fairness, and equal power.

To continue as we are—allowing selfish actors to control the rules and disrespect women—is to create a society where both men and women are trapped in unhealthy dynamics. But in a world where women are empowered, men will also have the opportunity to grow as true partners. They will no longer be saddled with unfair expectations of dominance, control, or sole responsibility for providing. Instead, they will stand alongside women, as equals, in creating families and futures that reflect the best of what humanity can offer.

When we fight for women's autonomy, we are also fighting for men's freedom to be true partners—partners who are not bound by old-fashioned, unequal roles but who are free to build strong, supportive, and fair households. This is a shared struggle, and in recognizing that, we build a future where both women and men can flourish. The health and future of this country depend on nothing less.

The erosion of bodily autonomy has weakened our families, disrupted our economy, and stunted our progress as a nation. The fight for autonomy is not only a moral one but a practical one: it will empower families, energize our economy, and restore justice. We envision a future where equality and freedom are more than lofty ideals; they are the foundation upon which a stronger, healthier, and more united America is built.

The American Ideals: Liberty and Equality for All

From the birth of our nation, Americans have prided themselves on being a people who value freedom above all else. Our Declaration of Independence states that all individuals are endowed with the inalienable rights of life, liberty, and the pursuit of happiness. But for centuries, half of our population—women—have been denied the most fundamental liberty: the right to control their own bodies. We must face the reality that the principles of liberty and justice have been incomplete and deeply flawed, creating a system that subjugates women and undermines their dignity.

In building a future where bodily autonomy is fully enshrined in law, we are not only correcting the wrongs of the past but realizing the true potential of America. A nation that respects the freedom and dignity of all its citizens is a nation that can thrive. This fight for autonomy must be seen as a continuation of the great civil rights struggles of our past, where marginalized groups fought for their place in society. Just as we overcame the legal disenfranchisement of women and people of color, we must now stand together to ensure that every person has control over their own body.

The founders of this country may have failed to fully realize the scope of liberty, but we have the opportunity to correct that failure. Enshrining bodily autonomy in our Constitution will guarantee that the fundamental right to self-determination is available to every American, not just a privileged few.

A Thriving Economy Through Gender Equality

In addition to being a moral imperative, gender equality and bodily autonomy are economic necessities. The old notion that inequality benefits business is based on flawed logic. For too long, businesses have exploited the gender gap, paying women less, offering minimal maternity benefits, and punishing women for taking time off to raise children. These practices may have appeared to boost profits in the short term, but they are damaging the long-term competitiveness and productivity of American businesses.

The evidence is clear: companies that embrace gender equality—where women are paid fairly, supported through family leave policies, and given equal opportunities for leadership—are more innovative, more productive, and more profitable. In countries that have prioritized gender equality, such as those in Scandinavia, businesses have flourished, and the economy has grown stronger. These nations have created environments where work-life balance is prioritized, women's contributions are valued, and families are supported, resulting in some of the happiest and most prosperous societies in the world.

The data speaks for itself. Companies with diverse workforces and equitable policies report better financial performance, higher employee satisfaction, and lower turnover rates. The inclusion of women in leadership positions has been shown to improve decision-making, foster innovation, and open up new markets. When women succeed, businesses succeed. This is a fact that American corporations can no longer afford to ignore.

157

By investing in gender equality—by offering paid family leave, closing the gender pay gap, and ensuring that women have equal opportunities for advancement—American businesses can unlock the full potential of their workforce. In doing so, they will not only boost their own bottom lines but contribute to a stronger, more competitive economy.

Rebuilding the American Family

At the heart of this struggle is the American family. For too long, traditional gender roles and systemic inequality have placed unfair burdens on women, creating imbalanced family structures and increasing levels of stress and unhappiness. The expectation that women must sacrifice their careers and personal ambitions for the sake of family, while men are pressured to be sole providers, has resulted in broken homes, rising divorce rates, and widespread dissatisfaction. These outdated ideals no longer serve the modern family.

In a society where bodily autonomy is fully respected, families will thrive. Gender equality will allow both partners in a relationship to share responsibilities more equitably, creating a balanced and supportive environment. When women have control over their reproductive choices, and men are empowered to participate equally in caregiving, the family unit becomes stronger and more resilient. Children raised in homes where both parents share in the responsibilities of work and family tend to fare better emotionally, academically, and socially.

Rebuilding the American family through equality will benefit not just women, but men and children as well. Men will no longer bear the sole burden of providing for their families, and they will have the freedom to fully participate in raising their children. Families will no longer be constrained by rigid gender roles but will be free to build relationships based on mutual respect, shared values, and equal partnership. This is the future we must fight for—a future where families are free to thrive without the weight of inequality holding them back.

The Moral Imperative: Justice for All

This fight for bodily autonomy is not just about women's rights—it is about justice for all. A society that respects the autonomy of every individual is a society that values justice, fairness, and equality. The denial of bodily autonomy has perpetuated systems of oppression and discrimination, keeping women, particularly women of color, trapped in cycles of poverty, inequality, and limited opportunities. This is not only unjust, but it is a profound failure of our moral and democratic values.

We are reminded of past struggles for equality—whether it was the fight for women's suffrage or the civil rights movement—where ordinary people stood up against injustice and changed the course of history. We are standing on the shoulders of these movements, and we must continue their work by fighting for bodily autonomy and gender equality. This is not just about reproductive rights or pay equity—it is about creating a world where every person is free to live with dignity, where their choices are respected, and where their potential is fully realized.

The fight for autonomy and equality will not just benefit women. It will create a society where men are no longer conditioned to dominate but to partner, where businesses thrive because they respect and support their employees, and where families grow stronger through mutual respect and shared responsibility. This is the moral imperative that will guide us into the future.

A Vision for the Future: A Stronger, United America

We stand at a pivotal moment in history. Imagine a future where every American has the right to control their own body, where men and women stand as equals in their homes, their workplaces, and their communities. A future where businesses thrive because they have unlocked the full potential of their workforce, where families are built on love and partnership, and where our economy grows stronger because it values the contributions of all its citizens.

This future is within our reach. Enshrining bodily autonomy in the U.S. Constitution will guarantee that no one —regardless of gender—can have their rights taken away. It will create a stronger, more resilient economy, healthier families, and a more just society. The benefits of this revolution will ripple through every aspect of our lives, lifting our nation up and ensuring that the promise of America is realized for all.

The fight for bodily autonomy and gender equality is a fight for a better future—a future where every individual is free to pursue their dreams, live with dignity, and build a life of their choosing. This is not just a women's issue—it is an American issue. It is time to act, to demand the change we deserve, and to build a society where freedom, justice, and equality are not just ideals but realities.

This is not merely a movement for women—it is a movement to enshrine and protect the most fundamental of human rights: the natural right to one's own body. This is about safeguarding the dignity and autonomy that every person is born with, the inalienable right to control their own being throughout their life. It is not just a matter of women's rights, but of human rights. If a person is not free to make decisions about their own body, then the promise of freedom and liberty that has been proclaimed for over two centuries is a hollow one. Such a denial turns individuals into subjects of the state rather than citizens of a free nation.

True freedom must begin with the body, for it is the vessel of our autonomy and the foundation of our personal sovereignty. Without this freedom, the very notion of liberty becomes an illusion—a broken promise never fully realized. This movement calls upon all Americans, men and women alike, to reclaim the rights that belong to them as individuals. Whether you believe in a creator or in your own inherent dignity, the right to control one's own body is sacred and must be protected for all. This is a right we must claim, not just for ourselves, but for everyone in our society.

Today we must start by drafting an amendment that will deprive the United States Government of all ownership over the bodies of the people. We must have an amendment that promises that our bodies are as projected from the injustices of law and despotism and abuse of the government against us. We are the property of our country. Our bodies, man and woman, are the possession of the government to make decisons over. Our bodies are NOT procected by the Constitution as stated firmly by the Supreme Court. If your body is the property of your government to do with as it pleases, you are objectively NOT free, you are a slave to your government. You are their property to do with however they rule in their laws. We must have an Amendment.

Together, we can rebuild America. Together, we can create a future where every person is free to live their life with dignity, respect, and equality. This is the promise of America, and it is a promise we must fulfill. The time for action is now, and the future is ours to build.

www.ingramcontent.com/pod-product-compliance
Lightning Source LLC
Chambersburg PA
CBHW051611250726

48653CB00004BA/1445